EXPERIENCING DEBUSSY

The Listener's Companion
Gregg Akkerman, Series Editor

Titles in **The Listener's Companion** provide readers with a deeper understanding of key musical genres and the work of major artists and composers. Aimed at nonspecialists, each volume explains in clear and accessible language how to *listen* to works from particular artists, composers, and genres. Looking at both the context in which the music first appeared and has since been heard, authors explore with readers the environments in which key musical works were written and performed.

EXPERIENCING DEBUSSY

A Listener's Companion

Teresa Davidian

ROWMAN & LITTLEFIELD
Lanham • Boulder • New York • London

Published by Rowman & Littlefield
An imprint of The Rowman & Littlefield Publishing Group, Inc.
4501 Forbes Boulevard, Suite 200, Lanham, Maryland 20706
www.rowman.com

Unit A, Whitacre Mews, 26-34 Stannary Street, London SE11 4AB

British Library Cataloguing in Publication Information Available

Library of Congress Cataloging-in-Publication Data

Names: Davidian, Teresa Maria, 1956– author.
Title: Experiencing Debussy : a listener's companion / Teresa Davidian.
Description: Lanham : Rowman & Littlefield, [2019] | Series: The listener's companion | Includes bibliographical references and index.
Identifiers: LCCN 2018026447 | ISBN 9781442271456 (cloth : alk. paper)
Subjects: LCSH: Debussy, Claude, 1862–1918—Criticism and interpretation.
Classification: LCC ML410.D28 D28 2019 | DDC 780.92—dc23
LC record available at https://lccn.loc.gov/2018026447

∞ ™ The paper used in this publication meets the minimum requirements of American National Standard for Information Sciences Permanence of Paper for Printed Library Materials, ANSI/NISO Z39.48-1992.

Printed in the United States of America

With love to my mother, Marie Thomasine Davidian, for putting me on the path that led to a life in music.

CONTENTS

SERIES EDITOR'S FOREWORD

The goal of the Listener's Companion series is to give readers a deeper understanding of pivotal musical genres and the creative work of its iconic composers and performers. This is accomplished in an inclusive manner that does not necessitate extensive music training or elitist shoulder rubbing. Authors of the series place the reader in specific listening experiences in which the music is examined in its historical context with regard to both compositional and societal parameters. By positioning the reader in the real or supposed environment of the music's creation, the author provides for a deeper enjoyment and appreciation of the art form. Series authors, often drawing on their own expertise as both performers and scholars, deliver to readers a broad understanding of major musical genres and the achievements of artists within those genres as lived listening experiences.

Like the man himself, the music of Claude Debussy is enigmatic. Water, the element that transfixed the composer and became a subject for many of his compositions, could serve as an emblem of Debussy's aesthetic: Surface tension masking content both subtle and powerful, translucency alternating with transparency, and a flow that allows for continually shifting and infinitely variable shapes. Water is always the same and always different, a characteristic applicable to Debussy's uncanny weaving of duplication and contrast. This volume addresses the slippery subject of the composer's unique compositional method throughout.

And if writing about Debussy's creative process is akin to grabbing a fistful of water, placing him in historical context is no less daunting. Debussy thrived at a moment in Western music history when all the chips were on the table. The system of major and minor scales, which had defined classical music for centuries, was eroding under the spell of Wagner and his manipulation of ambiguous harmonies. This laid a challenge before the composers who followed: Whence tonality? How much more might tonality be stretched before it broke? And just how should it be stretched? A whole raft of early twentieth-century composers answered these questions in different ways. Bartok turned to the exotic scales and rhythms of East European folk music, Stravinsky to polytonality and the austere symmetry of the octatonic scale, and Schoenberg to an ever-deepening atonality that eventually issued in his twelve-tone system. Debussy's path was far more subtle, and his relationship to Wagner's heritage more complex. As you will shortly discover, Debussy at first embraced Wagner, later to find in his music "a sunset mistaken for a dawn," as he famously put it.

Finally, there is the matter of the extreme popularity of certain isolated Debussy compositions, especially the ubiquitous "Clair de Lune," but including also a number of student and salon-style pieces that have made their way into popular culture and consciousness. Their familiarity serves almost to obscure the enormity of the composer's output, and to overrepresent him at the cost of other works' obscurity. The musical comedian Victor Borge used to illustrate this with a bit about a concert-goer who falls asleep during Debussy's *Suite bergamasque*, comes suddenly awake when she hears "Clair de Lune" (the suite's third movement)—and then falls fast asleep again when the last movement arrives.

In coming to grips with all these elements, Dr. Teresa Davidian has not exactly made for herself a simple task. That she accomplishes it with clarity, depth, and engagement owes to her combination of passion for the subject and masterful scholarship. She reveals to us her early enthusiasm for Debussy and her continuing love of his rich repertoire of orchestral, keyboard, vocal, and chamber-music works, and even shares with us that the scherzo of Debussy's String Quartet was played at her wedding reception. Debussy is personal for her, as well as professional. Davidian's academic background is in music theory, which makes her particularly well situated to understand and convey to the average reader the composer's compositional attitudes, habits, and eccentricities.

She makes good use of Debussy's own writings (like Robert Schumann, Debussy did a stint as music critic) and of the observations of the composer's contemporaries and champions. Always, Davidian manages to explain the music's inner workings in language available to the non-musician.

In the first chapter, we will meet "Clair de Lune" in all its iconic glory, along with Debussy's sole string quartet. In the second, we'll get to know the work that many classical music scholars consider the first truly modern score in music history, Debussy's *Prelude to "The Afternoon of a Faun,"* and will come to understand the composer less as an Impressionist than as a Symbolist. Chapter 3 examines at length the work that put Debussy on the cultural map, even though in the English-speaking world it is today largely forgotten: the composer's only completed opera, *Pelléas et Mélisande.* Many will find chapter 4 surprising for detailing the differences—musical and personal—between Debussy and the composer with whom he is often paired, Maurice Ravel. Debussy's aforementioned fascination with H_2O is addressed in chapter 5's look at *La mer*; his French nationalism opens the door to a range of works in chapter 6, and chapter 7 both grapples with one of the composer's most difficult and forward-looking scores, *Jeux,* and returns us full circle to the pop-culture appropriation of Debussy in such varied places as Hitchcock's *The Birds* and the dramatic cable series *Westworld.*

Until now, Debussy to you may have meant "Clair de Lune." After reading Davidian's book, he will continue to mean that but will mean much, much more as well.

Kenneth LaFave

INTRODUCTION

Claude Debussy was one of the most truly original figures in the transition from nineteenth- to twentieth-century art music. Such works as his *Prélude à "L'Après-midi d'un faune"* (*Prelude to "The Afternoon of a Faun"*) and *La mer* (*The Sea*) represent distinct breaks with nineteenth-century musical styles and forms. The *Prelude to "The Afternoon of a Faun,"* in particular, has been hailed by Pierre Boulez and later generations of composers as a seminal work in the development of twentieth-century music. With its languid melodies, subtle gradations of dynamics and texture, and fluid tempos, this 1894 work is the overt antithesis to Wagner's weighty and intense music dramas, which Debussy viewed collectively as a "marshy stench."

Debussy's first group of supporters were the "Debussystes," who championed the composer during the controversial premiere and ultimate success of *Pelléas et Mélisande* in 1902. It was this work, his one and only completed opera, that helped open the doors for a professional career and brought attention to his other compositions. Within a few years after the premiere, he was among the most celebrated composers in all of France. His fame quickly spread throughout Europe as well as to other countries and continents, as is evident by the considerable number of performance reviews, interviews, and articles published in the years following *Pelléas et Mélisande*. One example is an interview with the composer that appeared in the December 6, 1910, issue of a Hungarian evening newspaper:

> For two days the most illustrious representative of French music—
> her poet, apostle, and prophet—has been here in Budapest. This
> illustrious visitor goes by the name of Claude Debussy. He is still a
> young man but he has already acquired immortality—something not
> gained by passing glory, nor lasting success, but the foremost heri-
> tage of genius. Debussy has enriched music with new impressions,
> sentiments, and effects. And the importance of his poetic utterance
> is heightened by the fact that it is perhaps more than the mere
> grandiose ideas and novelties of one man alone: it shows the whole
> tendency of French music in a state of renewal, advancing toward an
> eclipse of the triumphant Wagnerism that resounds within it.

In the hundred years since his death in 1918, interest in Debussy's
music has never ceased. There have been numerous recordings of his
music, films, dissertations, and scholarly books and papers—all attesting
to the significance and fascination with Debussy as an artist. Highlights
of the latest research topics, which will be presented at an international
conference in Manchester and Glasgow in 2018, include his multiple
use of the triptych format, his wartime works, the reception history of
his music in Japan and China, and the components of his legacy. My
own research began with a study of his sonata forms, with special reference to the *Fantaisie* for piano and orchestra, the String Quartet, and
the three late sonatas. In connection with my doctoral work in the
1980s, I wish to circle back in time and thank again the French commu-
nity of Debussy scholars and supporters for their help and guidance
during this early phase of my career, especially François Lesure, Myri-
am Chimènes, and Denis Herlin in Paris; and Madame Henri Gouin at
the Abbaye de Royaumont north of Paris.

While I subsequently explored other music and composers, I always
wanted to return my focus to Debussy—hence this book. In writing it,
my overall aim is to enrich the reader's understanding and admiration
of this remarkable musician. What I think will emerge during the
course of my book is a complex and multivalent picture of Debussy. A
true artist, his music does not fit neatly into a particular "ism" but
manifests ties to many: Impressionism, Symbolism, exoticism, neoclassicism, and nationalism. In addition to this complex web of connections, I
explore a few themes that persisted in his compositional output, such as
water, nature, and stories by Edgar Allan Poe.

Altogether, I discuss approximately thirty works in a loose chronological order. Whenever possible, I include Debussy's own words, as expressed in his private letters and published articles. They are an excellent source for biographical data and provide insights into his character and personality. They also give direct evidence of his position on a wide variety of topics, ranging from his admiration of the music of Johann Sebastian Bach to his hatred of being labeled an Impressionist and his hopes for the future.

As his many music reviews attest, Debussy is one of the most incisive music critics of his time. While a master of the low, clean, and direct hit, he could also be funny and charming. His first articles, dating from spring 1901, appeared in *La Revue blanche* (The White Review), a monthly magazine that was published in Paris from 1891 to 1903. His later writings, consisting of reviews and articles on a variety of topics, were for *Gil Blas*, *Musica*, *Le Figaro*, *Le Matin*, and the Société internationale de musique (SIM), to name just a few. Some essays he wrote under the pseudonym "Monsieur Croche," which might be translated as Mr. Quaver or Mr. Eighth Note. Indeed, some of his most crotchety essays appear under the pseudonym "Monsieur Croche."

Regarding my quotations from Debussy's articles and letters, I frequently relied on two sources: *Debussy Letters*, edited by François Lesure and Roger Nichols; and *Debussy on Music* collected by François Lesure and translated and edited by Richard Langham Smith. I cite these sources within the text as *Letters* and *DOM*, respectively. In general, while I do not use footnotes and keep citations to a minimum, the sources of my information and ideas can be found in the bibliography.

Interspersed within the following narrative are my own experiences with Debussy's music, as both a performer and scholar. They supplement the more generalized statements as well as enable me to connect more closely with readers. It is my hope that my own deep feelings for Debussy will translate into a trigger for the reader as well. This is because actual feeling—and not the description of feeling—is at the heart of his aesthetic. "Music, don't you know," he wrote in a letter to André Poniatowski in February 1893, "is a dream from which the veils have been lifted. It's not even the expression of a feeling, it's the feeling itself" (*Letters*, 41).

TIMELINE

1862   Born August 22 at Saint-Germain-en-Laye to Manuel-Achille Debussy and Victorine Manoury Debussy.

1867   Debussy family settles in Paris.

1872   Enters Paris Conservatoire on October 22.

1874   Wins third prize for solfège at the Paris Conservatoire. Wins honorable mention for performing Chopin's Second Piano Concerto.

1875   Wins second medal for solfège and first honorable mention for performing Chopin's first *ballade*.

1876   First public appearance on January 16. Wins first medal for solfège.

1877   Wins second prize in piano for performing Schumann's Sonata in G minor.

1878   Fails to win any prizes at the Conservatoire.

1880   Wins first prize in piano accompaniment. Hired as a piano accompanist for Nadezhda von Meck, a wealthy patroness of Tchaikovsky, from July 20 through November 5. Meets Blanche Vasnier.

1881   With Mme. von Meck from mid-July to the beginning of December.

1882   Plays own music for first time in public on May 12 ("Fête galante" and "Les Roses"). First original work published in June: *Nuit d'étoiles*. With Mme. von Meck and her entourage from September 8 through the end of September.

1883   Wins second prize in Prix de Rome competition (May 19 through June 13).

1884   Wins first prize in Prix de Rome competition (May 24 through June 18).

1885   Goes to Rome to live and study in the Villa Medici for an expected stay of two years. After receiving a leave of absence from the Villa Medici on July 8, he stays in Dieppe with Marie Vasnier. Returns to Rome in September.

1886   Leaves Rome and returns to Paris for the summer.

1887   Completes *Printemps*, which is harshly criticized by the Institut. Leaves Rome for good on March 2.

1888   *Ariettes oubliées* is published in January. Joins the Société nationale de musique. Travels to Bayreuth in August; hears *Parsifal* and *Die Meistersinger*. Begins *Deux arabesques*.

1889   First performance of *Petite Suite* for piano duet. Attends Universal Exhibition in Paris in June and July. Travels to Bayreuth in August; hears *Tristan und Isolde*.

1890   Publishes *Cinq Poèmes de Baudelaire* in February. Begins opera *Rodrigue et Chimène*, which he will abandon in 1892. Begins *Suite bergamasque*, which will not be published until 1905. Composes *Rêverie*.

1891   Meets Erik Satie. Begins to compose the first set of *Fêtes galantes*.

1892   Meets Gabrielle (Gaby) Dupont.

1893   Is elected to the committee of the Société nationale de musique on April 23. Begins to set Maeterlinck's play *Pelléas et Mélisande* to music. First performance of the String Quartet on December 29.

1894   Becomes engaged to singer Thérèse Roger in February; engagement broken off in March. First performance of *Prélude à "L'Après-midi d'un faune"* on December 22.

1895   Finishes first version of *Pelléas et Mélisande* in August. *Proses lyriques* published.

1897   Gaby attempts suicide in February. Premiere of Debussy's orchestral setting of the first and third movements of Satie's *Gymnopédies* on February 20. Begins *Trois Chansons de Bilitis* in June.

1898   Hears Ravel's "Habanera" at a Société nationale de musique concert on March 5. Breaks up with Gabrielle Dupont.

1899   By spring, Debussy is seeing Marie-Rosalie (Lilly) Texier. They marry on October 19. Finishes *Nocturnes*.

1900   "Nuages" and "Fêtes," the first and second movement of *Nocturnes*, are performed on December 9.

1901   Becomes music critic for *La Revue blanche* in April. Monsieur Croche appears in the July 1 issue. All three movements of *Nocturnes* are performed on October 27.

1902   First performance of *Pour le piano* on January 11. First performance of *Pelléas et Mélisande* on April 30. The opera makes Debussy an overnight sensation.

1903   Is made Chevalier of the Legion of Honor in January. Publishes twenty-six articles for *Gil Blas* between January and June. Meets Emma Bardac. Begins *La mer* and completes *Estampes*.

1904   First performance of *Estampes* on January 9. Dedicates *Fêtes galantes*, series 2, to Emma in June. In August, he runs away with Emma to Jersey and coastal towns in Normandy, where they will stay until mid-October. While in Normandy, he revises *L'isle joyeuse*, which he had begun the year before, and *Masques*. Lilly attempts suicide with a revolver on October 13.

1905   First performance of *L'isle joyeuse* and *Masques* on February 10. Emma and husband Sigismund Bardac are divorced on May 4, Debussy and Lilly on August 2. First performance of *La mer* on October 15. Birth of Claude-Emma Debussy, known as Chouchou, on October 30.

1906   Piano *Images*, series 1, performed on February 6. Composes "Ibéria," to become the second movement of *Images* for orchestra.

1907   Works on "Rondes de printemps," the third movement of the *Images* for orchestra.

1908   Marries Emma Bardac on January 20. Sells performance rights to the Metropolitan Opera in New York for two one-act operas based on Edgar Allan Poe's *Devil in the Belfry* and *Fall of the House of Usher*. *Children's Corner* is performed on December 23.

1909   Is appointed to the advisory board of the Conservatoire. Conducts *Prélude à "L'Après-midi d'un faune"* in London on February 27. First biography of Debussy, by Louis Laloy, is published in September. Composes *Rapsodie* for clarinet for a Conservatoire contest in December. The *Préludes* for piano, book 1, also date from this time.

1910   "Ibéria," the central movement of the *Images* for orchestra, is performed. Meets Stravinsky in June. First hearing of *Trois ballades de François Villon* in November in London.

1911   First performance of *Le martyre de Saint Sebastien* on May 22. Conducts in Turin.

1912   Premiere of the ballet *L'Après-midi d'un faune*, performed by the Ballets Russes on May 29.

1913   First performance of the three *Images* for orchestra on January 26. *Préludes*, book 2, published April 19. Ballet *Jeux* performed by Ballets Russes on May 15. Premiere of *Syrinx* on December 1. Conducts in Moscow and St. Petersburg in December at the invitation of Koussevitsky.

1914   Conducts in Rome and Amsterdam in February. Gives last interview in May.

1915   Mother Victorine dies in March. Composes *En blanc et noir* (June), Sonata for Cello and Piano, *Douze Etudes*, Sonata for

Flute, Viola, and Harp, and *Noël des enfants qui n'ont plus de maison*. Undergoes operation for rectal cancer in December.

1916   Premieres of *En blanc et noir* on January 22, the Sonata for Flute, Viola, and Harp on December 10. Begins Sonata for Violin and Piano. First performance of the *Douze Etudes* on November 10 at Aeolian Hall in New York.

1917   Makes last public appearance as a performer with violinist Gaston Poulet on May 5. They perform the Sonata for Violin and Piano at a Société nationale de musique concert at the Salle Gaveau.

1918   Dies from cancer on March 25 in Paris, aged fifty-five.

1919   Chouchou dies from diphtheria on July 16.

THE EARLY YEARS

Rebel and Insider

"Clair de Lune," by French composer Claude Debussy, is one of the most recognizable examples of classical music in the Western world. This piece, which translates into English as "Moonlight," can be heard in many different media—from films to plays, from pop songs to TV shows and cartoons, and from video games to commercials and even an animated Google Doodle. Did you see this particular Doodle? It appeared on the Google home page on August 22, 2013, in commemoration of the influential composer's 151st birthday. This Doodle can still be accessed today. Visually, it features a moody night scene in Paris by the River Seine. A full moon, flickering stars, streetlights, and the puffs of smoke from chimneys—all these images are synced with the opening section of Debussy's "Clair de Lune." Adding to the dreamy, nostalgic quality of the clip are vintage cars and a bicycle slowly making their way along the quai, the subtle colors dominated by gray and blue, and the operating windmill and balloons. Toward the end of this brief tableau, which lasts a little over two minutes, it starts to rain, and the Doodle ends with silhouettes of a man and a woman in separate rowboats stopping to share a bright red umbrella. This elegant "Clair de Lune" Doodle is sometimes considered one of the best moments in the entire eighteen-year history of Google, which has of course the top Internet search engine in the world.

Debussy began writing "Clair de Lune" as a piano work in 1890, when he was twenty-eight years old, but he did not complete or publish it until 1905. Subsequently, it was orchestrated by his friend André Caplet, a masterful composer in his own right, in 1924, six years after Debussy's death. Since the 1930s, the work has maintained a steady media presence across the decades. For instance, it has been featured in dozens of films, such as *Bolero* (1934), *Portrait of Jennie* (1948), *Giant* (1956), *Casino Royale* (1967), *Castaway* (1986), *Frankie and Johnny* (1991), *Twilight* (2008), and *American Hustle* (2013). There is even a beautiful rendition by the great Larry Adler on harmonica in the 1944 movie *Music for Millions*.

WHAT IS IT ABOUT "CLAIR DE LUNE"?

Why has "Clair de Lune" resonated so pervasively and persistently in media for nearly a century? In my opinion, there is not one single reason for the work's popularity but a combination of sound qualities. In just the opening of the piece, the combination consists of drawing together light, space, free-floating movement, and subtle mystery.

With regard to the quality of lightness, the first few notes are played very softly (*pianissimo* and *con sordina*) and in a high range. There are no notes sounding below middle C on the piano, perhaps because they would potentially weigh down the music floating on high. Almost immediately, though, the music proceeds to sink slowly, step by step, with the lower (left-hand) part leading the way, dragging the higher (right-hand) part along into the lower depths. By the time the music reaches the end of a two-octave descent, the left hand detaches from the right-hand part and dives down to an even lower depth, only to reverse course quickly and bounce gracefully back up to a restatement of the very opening of the piece. This time, the music proceeds on surer ground since the main melody now has a fuller and expanded accompaniment. In a sense, the sequence of events that describe the opening of "Clair de Lune" brings to mind what some of us experience after a long, hard day at work: when we get home, we start to relax and decompress, sinking into a comfortable couch and drifting off to sleep. But just as we fall asleep, our bodies spring awake and we return to consciousness.

The quality of spaciousness is especially evident about midway through the "Clair de Lune" Doodle. This is when we hear a series of very soft octaves, beginning on the lower end of the piano keyboard, alternating with chords sounding on high. The distance between the octaves and chords spans more than three octaves; there are no notes in the middle range to fill in the space. It is as if Debussy is trying to convey in musical terms the wide expanse between the ground and the moonlit sky.

On the other hand, a floating quality can be discerned throughout the entire clip and is tied to Debussy's distinctive use of rhythm. A comparison to a more familiar rhythmic pattern will help clarify this point. Think of a marching rhythm: HUP-two-three-four, HUP-two-three-four, and so forth. It is so strong and repetitive we can easily tap or move our feet to it. In "Clair de Lune," by contrast, we cannot tap to it beat by beat. Trust me, the rhythm in this piece can be extremely challenging to decipher. As a teenager, I spent hours trying to count out the rhythm. Whenever I gave up and just tried to approximate the music by ear, my teacher would quickly pounce and instruct me to count out loud. A hard lesson learned: Debussy's music may sound free and loose, but it is carefully constructed.

Without getting too technical, Debussy's rhythms in the Doodle clip are frequently syncopated; his notes often occur "off the beat." Consequently, his music sounds rhythmically free, with notes gently floating over the beat. The sustained chords at the ends of measures along with the slow tempo also hold back any sense of forward momentum and urgency. Unlike a work like Beethoven's Fifth Symphony, which is distinguished by a powerful, driving rhythmic motif (ta-ta-ta-daaa), Debussy's "Clair de Lune" has the exact opposite effect.

Finally, there is a sense of mystery that infuses the work, due in large part to Debussy's unique harmonic style. His harmonies are not always straightforward and clear; rather, they can be ambiguous. In technical terms, Debussy begins with sonorities that have no root or anchor (also known as a type of incomplete chord). He then writes chains of inverted chords wherein the roots are shifted from the traditional bass position to a rather hidden inner part. In fact, only two of the eighteen chords heard in the Doodle clip are in the stronger root position. The first occurs when the white and yellow lights of the ship appear, and the second at the end of the clip, when the woman unfurls a red umbrella.

Interestingly, the creator of the Google Doodle, Leon Hong, hit upon a visual representation of "Clair de Lune" that neatly coincides with the harmonic design. Muted grays and blues predominate while the primary colors of yellow and red are reserved for the main arrival points of the musical excerpt.

Contributing to the mysterious mood of the work is a lack of exact repetition of material, which normally serves as a signpost in music. Notice that the one time when the opening melody does recur in the Doodle (i.e., when the ship lights appear), it has a thicker and deeper accompaniment. In fact, in the remainder of the piece, whenever the main melody recurs, there is always something different about its accompaniment. Debussy is a master of this type of variation: he will begin with just a hint of melody, as opposed to one that is fully formed, and then subsequently return to it, sometimes more firmly, other times with a subtler change. In effect, he is creating the musical equivalent of a recurring dream wherein no two dreams in a series are the same; just the theme stays the same.

The above is just one of several possible explanations of "Clair de Lune." To be sure, there is no definitive reading of the piece, nor a singular path to understanding Debussy's music in general. This is because his music defies neat categorization and is generally resistant to analysis. He himself deliberately cultivated mystery and ambiguity in his works. Nor did he want the general public to know his secrets and methods of composition. This statement can be corroborated by some of his critical writings that appeared in a number of French newspapers and periodicals of the time, including *Le Figaro, Intransigeant, Le Matin, Mercure de France*, and *La Revue blanche*. Consider his review of a performance at the Concerts Lamoreux, which appeared in *Gil Blas* on February 23, 1903:

> I would like to protest against a custom that is prevalent each time a modern symphony is performed: that is, that a four-page thematic analysis containing the text as well as numerous illustrative examples is distributed among the audience. It tells everyone how a composer should treat his theme, and puts the secrets of composing a symphony at the disposal of the public. There is nothing to prevent the dilettante listener from being attracted to the idea of composing his own little symphony! Being unable to contain himself, he might even take it, still warm, to M. Chevillard [the conductor of the Orchestre

Lamoureux]. It's an encouragement to all the horrors of the symphony. Moreover, I believe that it is dangerous to initiate laymen into the secrets of musical chemistry. Some people do treat these little analyses with suspicion, as it they were explosive, others treat them with a puzzled stupefaction, but the most sensible people send them gently away on the north wind, or quite simply put them in their pockets—and there is the real moral of the story.

From the above quote, we might conclude that Debussy was a bit of a snob. This may be indeed true, but the composer's stance on concert-hall audiences could also be understood as a reflection of the time. In terms of history, Debussy was a transitional figure between late romantic and modern eras of music, and one aspect of romanticism was the idea of the composer as an artist, a divine genius, rather than a craftsman or someone who creates things to make sense. It appears that Debussy regarded himself on the godlike side of the continuum. It could be argued that we, his admirers today, should respect his wishes and refrain from uncovering the secrets of his art. But for those of us who enjoy the process of trying to solve a challenging puzzle or finding all the clues to a good mystery, Debussy's music will always be intriguing and fascinating. I myself am the daughter and sister of mechanics and the niece and cousin of mechanical engineers. Like them, I enjoy figuring out how things work. Throughout my professional career as a music theorist and musicologist, I have been drawn to the structural aspects of Debussy's music. I do not think that I am disrespecting Debussy by analyzing his music. If anything, I have gained a greater appreciation of his art and skill, as well as greater insight to the inner workings of his masterpieces. I have found that he is not, as many of his detractors have argued, just a pretty, lightweight composer. Rather, like Mozart, Debussy's music is carefully crafted and designed beneath an elegant surface.

With his later works, Debussy showed that his "Clair de Lune" was not a one-off success. They, too, have been performed again and again for more than a century and include his String Quartet (1893), a one-movement orchestral tone poem called *Prelude to "The Afternoon of a Faun"* (1894), and the opera *Pelléas et Mélisande*. Yet in many respects, "Clair de Lune" is emblematic of Debussy's style. Before taking an even closer look at this piece, it would be worthwhile to bring the composer into better focus.

AN UNLIKELY BEGINNING FOR A GREAT FRENCH COMPOSER

Claude Debussy was an unlikely person to write some of the most beautiful pieces in the classical repertoire. First of all, he grew up in a family of very modest means. His father Manuel (1836–1910) tried his hand at several different jobs to keep his family of seven fed. He ran a china shop with his wife Victorine Manoury (1836–1915), became a traveling salesman, and worked as a bookkeeper, to name just three jobs. Nor is there any evidence indicating that Debussy had a musical background from which to draw. We know that his only sister, Adèle (1863–1852), became a seamstress; in a 1909 interview, she stated that she had "no sympathy" with her brother's compositions. Of his three younger brothers, Emmanuel (1867–1937) got a job in Paris as a "scavenger of cesspools" and later became a farmhand. Alfred (1870–1937) worked as an inspector for a French railway company and was reported to have frequented music halls. The youngest brother, Eugène (1873–1877), died from meningitis in spring 1877 at the age of three.

So how did a poor French boy, who was born into an essentially nonmusical family, grow up to become the most famous French composer of all time? His ticket out of poverty was his musical talent, plain and simple. Several people noticed this talent when he was very young. In 1870, when he was seven years old, his aunt Clémentine Debussy arranged for him to take piano lessons with a musician in Cannes, which must have seemed like an extravagance to his struggling parents. The following year, he continued to take piano lessons, this time with Antoinette Mauté, who claimed to have studied with Chopin. It was Madame Mauté who decided that the young Debussy had the talent to succeed at the Conservatoire national superior de musique, aka the Paris Conservatory. Thanks to her first-rate tutelage, he was accepted after competitive examination to the prestigious institution just one year later. Since Debussy got into the best music school in France after only two years of music lessons, a short of period of time, we can deduce that he must have been good.

AT THE CONSERVATOIRE

Debussy studied at the Paris Conservatoire for the next eleven years, where he generally excelled. One distinguishing feature of the school was its prize system, which meant that students had to receive a first prize on their major instrument in order to receive a certificate or diploma. Debussy did win the top medals in two music subjects: solfège in 1876 and accompanying in 1880. However, he never received the top medal for piano, his primary instrument. The highest award he obtained was second place in 1877 for his performance of Schumann's Sonata in G minor, op. 22. Because he failed to win the top prize in piano after several attempts, he could no longer pursue a career as a piano virtuoso. He had to think of another career path. By 1879, he had decided to become a composer, and his first songs date from this time. The following year, he began formal composition study. His professor at the Paris Conservatoire was Ernest Guiraud (1837–1892), a French composer of *opéras comiques* who had studied with Georges Bizet and was born in New Orleans, Louisiana.

Although Debussy's career as a solo pianist was effectively over by 1880, his teachers at the Conservatoire continued to believe in him and his musical abilities. This is not to say that he had been a model student; on the contrary, he had already gained a reputation as a rebel. According to eyewitness accounts, he had tried the patience of his harmony teacher Emile Durand by willfully breaking traditional rules of harmony, while outside of class he delighted his classmates by wildly improvising on his homework assignments.

Ernest Guiraud was the perfect teacher for a talented and wayward student like the young Debussy. Guiraud could be understanding and supportive, yet also firm and direct. As stated in his semester examination report of 1882, Guiraud gave the following assessment of his young student: "Some progress. Poorly balanced temperament, but intelligent. Will succeed, I believe." In 1883, after reading through a piece that Debussy had just finished writing, Guiraud gave him some wise and helpful counsel: "Well, all that's very interesting, but you must save it for later. Or else you will never win the Rome Prize." Guiraud's remarks here were reported by Louis Laloy, Debussy's first biographer, in 1910.

It appears that Debussy did follow Guiraud's advice. In 1884 he won the Rome Prize for music composition, the most prestigious prize for arts students in France and the final stage in the country's prize system. Then as now, this award is a much-coveted means to establish careers. Winners receive a scholarship to complete a subsidized, multiyear residency in Rome. The prize was originally created for visual artists during the reign of Louis XIV but was later expanded to include other arts; music was added in 1803. Debussy's own path to the prize was not particularly easy for he had entered the competition three years in a row, winning on the third try. However, he eventually succeeded where many other prominent composers did not. These include Camille Saint-Saëns, Ernest Chausson, Maurice Ravel, and Olivier Messiaen.

THE MENTORING OF DEBUSSY

Ernest Guiraud was not the only teacher at the Paris Conservatoire who helped to further Debussy's musical career. Another member of the faculty who stepped forward was his longtime piano teacher, Antoine Marmontel (1816–1898), who found enviable employment for Debussy. He arranged for Debussy to play piano in the summer of 1879 at the beautiful Château of Chenonceau, which spans the River Cher in the Loire Valley and which had been a favorite residence of Catherine de Medici. For an inner city youth like Debussy, whose large family currently lived in a three-room apartment, the Chenonceau estate must have seemed idyllic.

Marmontel found an even better job for Debussy for the following summer, when he recommended the eighteen-year-old musician to Nadezhda von Meck (1831–1894), the widow of a wealthy railway tycoon who made his fortune by expanding the railways in Russia. She is perhaps best known today as the arts patron who had a strange relationship with Tchaikovsky. While she supported the Russian composer with a monthly allowance for fourteen years, under the terms of their arrangement, they were not allowed to meet. Their strange relationship was conducted entirely through letters, of which approximately 1,200 survive. On the one occasion that Madame von Meck and Tchaikovsky happened to cross paths in person, they averted their eyes.

Her relationship with Debussy was very different since he was a member of her large entourage of children and servants. From July 20 to November 5, 1880, he traveled with them to sumptuous locales: first to Interlaken, Switzerland, then to the seaside town of Arcachon in southern France, and eventually to the Villa Oppenheim, overlooking the beautiful Boboli Gardens in Florence. His duties included giving piano lessons to her children, playing piano duets with Madame von Meck, and accompanying her daughter Julia in vocal recitals.

Like Debussy's teachers at the Conservatoire, Nadezhda von Meck was quite impressed with the young French musician. She rehired him for two additional long-term appointments. In July 1881, he rejoined her family and retinue, this time in Moscow, where he lived and worked for several months. That October, he traveled with them to Rome and back to Florence. In July 1882, he resided with the von Mecks at their country estate outside Moscow. This third and final stay with the von Mecks ended in Vienna in early fall 1882.

In addition to employing Debussy for three extended summer stays, von Meck promoted him to Tchaikovsky. In her letters to the great Russian composer, she praised Debussy's trenchant wit and gift for mimicry, as well as his brilliant playing technique and sight-reading ability. She even sent Tchaikovsky an original work by the young Debussy, entitled *Danse bohémienne*. According to Edward Lockspeiser in his 1936 article "Debussy, Tchaikovsky and Madame von Meck," Tchaikovsky thought that the Debussy piece was "a very nice little thing but altogether too short. Not a single thought is developed to the end, the form is bungled and there is no unity." It is not known if Madame von Meck reported back to Debussy. In any event, he never published the piece.

Thus, by the time Debussy arrived in Rome with the Prix de Rome in hand, he had achieved a great deal. He may have been born into a poor and nonmusical family, but he had climbed up the ladder of academic success. He had also secured several artist-in-residencies, thanks in part to the help of his teachers and a patron who believed in him. During his student years and throughout his travels abroad, he had invariably gained some knowledge of very diverse types of classical art music, including the scores of Wagner, Tchaikovsky, and other Russian composers. Such knowledge further enhanced his apprenticeship. Now he was set to embark on the next phase of his career: a minimum three-year residency in the Villa Medici in Rome, which commenced in 1884.

AT THE VILLA MEDICI

Many of us know well that the Spanish Steps are a popular tourist attraction in the center of Rome. As one of the longest and widest staircases in all of Europe, we have stopped at the landmark to meet and relax. The staircase has a rather unusual butterfly design, but it is the city view from the top that is truly spectacular. Not far from the top of the steps stands the beautiful Villa Medici, a sixteenth-century building named after Cardinal Ferdinando de' Medici (1549–1609), a member of the famous of Medici family of Florence and a grand duke of Tuscany. Flanking the villa is a panoramic garden with fountains, which has been described as one of the most beautiful parks in Italy.

But Debussy was absolutely miserable at the Villa Medici, especially when he arrived in the winter of 1885. In a single letter written in early February 1885 to Eugène Vasnier, another mentor and a famous art collector, Debussy complained about the weather: "Wind and rain. You must admit there was hardly any point coming to Rome to find the same weather we have in Paris." He complained that his former Parisian friends had become nasty competitors: "If you could only see how they're changed! No more of the friendliness of Paris." And he despised his cavernous dormitory room, which he was obliged to share with six other students: "Then back to my vast room, with a five mile walk between one piece of furniture and the next. I've been so lonely I've cried" (*Letters*, 5). Several months later, in another letter to Vasnier, he described the villa as "wretched barracks, where life is so miserable."

Debussy had good reason to complain about the Villa Medici. According to descriptions provided by Hector Berlioz and other Prix de Rome winners, the facilities were seriously lacking. Similar to Debussy, Berlioz described the accommodations as "stupid barracks." But it seems that the root of Debussy's general misery was loneliness. At that time, he was in love with Vasnier's beautiful wife, Marie-Blanche Vasnier (1848–1923), a soprano whom he had met back in 1880 and who was much older than Debussy. This married mother of two children was his muse. Because of her, he wrote approximately two dozen songs or *mélo-*

dies, some of which remained unpublished during his lifetime. Other *mélodies* were eventually published in a collection now known as the *Vasnier Songbook* and have become an essential part of the modern singers' repertoire. These include "Mandoline" (1882), "Romance: Silence ineffable de l'heure" (1885), and the six *Ariettes oubliées* (1886–1887).

It seems likely that Debussy wrote the Vasnier songs while staying at the Villa Medici. He composed other works of course, notably the envois expected of every Prix de Rome fellow. Envois were annual works that each Prix de Rome winner sent back to Paris to be judged by a jury at the Académie des Beaux-Arts, one of the five academies of the Institut de France. Debussy was supposed to write a total of four envois, but he only managed to complete two while in Rome—a symphonic ode called *Zuleima* in December 1885, and a wordless choral piece entitled *Printemps* in February 1887. *Zuleima* is a lost work, but we know what the judges thought about it: "Bizarre, incomprehensible, and impossible to perform." Henri Delaborde, the secretary of the Académie, provided this official assessment in 1886. The official review of *Printemps*, Debussy's second envoi, was not much better. It too included the word "bizarre." Delaborde's 1887 report is worth quoting here since it constitutes the first time that the word "impressionism" is associated with Debussy's music:

> M. Debussy assuredly does not transgress by platitude or banality. He has, quite to the contrary, a pronounced, even too pronounced, tendency toward the pursuit of the strange. One recognizes in his case a feeling for musical color, the exaggeration of which makes him too easily forget the importance of precision of design and form. It is strongly desired that he guard against this vague "impressionism" that is one of the most dangerous enemies of truth in works of art. The first movement of the symphonic piece of M. Debussy is a sort of adagio prelude, of a reverie and affectation that lead to confusion. The second movement is a bizarre and incoherent transformation of the first, which the combinations of the rhythm render at least a little clearer and more perceptible. The Académie expects and hopes for better from a musician as talented as M. Debussy.

Shortly after Delaborde's above assessment was published, Debussy left the Villa Medici in Rome for good and returned to his parents in Paris.

He had only completed the minimum two years of residence. Whether this rash decision had to do with his long-distance affair with Madam Vasnier, dissatisfaction with the facilities, or the harsh criticism he received for his two envois is not clear. (A combination of factors seems likely.) In any case, he quit after fulfilling only two of the requisite three years. For the record, he had spent even less time than that. During his Prix de Rome period in Italy, which began in January 1885 and ended in March 1887, he had applied for and received several extended leaves of absence. One of these was for a two-month vacation in Dieppe, a port on the coast of Normandy, with Madame Vasnier, possibly without her husband's knowledge.

Years later, Debussy had more positive things to say about the Villa Medici. In his 1903 article entitled "A Consideration of the Prix de Rome from a Musical Point of View," he fondly recalled the beauty of the Villa Medici: "One cannot but be moved when one remembers the wonderful trees surrounding the Villa Medici, fading away into the gentle violet of the Umbrian hills. The architecture of the loggia too, with its columns of purely decorative marble, brings back countless memories." On the other hand, in this same article he continued to criticize the substandard accommodations: "In the refectory there, one paid 1 franc 25 for a diet that ruined one's stomach for life!" He also contended that the award process was neither valid nor realistic: "The cool way in which the academic gentlemen of the Institute decide which of these young people shall be artists seems to me to be strikingly naïve. What do they know about it? How can they be so confident about controlling other people's destinies—something in which there is bound to be an element of chance?" A sad conclusion, which only serves to underline the uselessness of the Prix de Rome, at least insofar as achieving a kind of art that will testify to the beauty of our age.

BACK IN PARIS: A BOHEMIAN EXISTENCE

It was 1887. Debussy had fled Rome in February and moved back in with his family in Paris on rue de Berlin (later rue de Liège), located near the Gare St-Lazare. Relatively little is known about the next few years of his biography since letters dating from this period are scarce. We do know that he completed two additional Prix de Rome envois from Paris, a cantata called *La Damoiselle élue* in 1889, and the *Fantaisie* for piano and orchestra in 1890. He also produced a piano duet called *Petite Suite* (1887), started the *Deux arabesques* for solo piano (1888), and produced other works that are still performed to this day. And he started the *Suite bergamasque* for piano, of which "Clair de Lune" is part.

In retrospect, Debussy's experiences between his return from Rome in 1887 and the premiere of his first masterpiece, the *Prelude to "The Afternoon of a Faun,"* in 1894 had a profound effect on his later artistic development. During this seven-year period, he became infatuated with the music of Richard Wagner. In 1888 he took the first of two trips to Bayreuth to hear Wagner's *Parsifal* and *Die Meistersinger*, his trip made possible by Etienne Dupin, a wealthy acquaintance and patron of music. He took a second trip to Bayreuth the following year to hear *Tristan und Isolde*.

During this same period, he attended the 1889 World's Fair in Paris. While there, he was enthralled with the Javanese gamelan orchestra, which consisted of exotic metallophones, xylophones, drums, gongs, bamboo flutes, and strings. According to his friend Robert Godet, "Many fruitful hours for Debussy were spent in the Javanese *kampong* [village] of the Dutch section listening to the percussive rhythmic complexities of the gamelan with its inexhaustible combination of ethereal, flashing timbres." For many scholars, Javanese music influenced the way Debussy was later to compose.

Essentially, however, he led the life of a bohemian artist. He went to the famous *Chat noir* cabaret where his friend Erik Satie performed as a second pianist. He frequented smoky Paris cafes, such as the Brasserie Pousset in Montmartre, and absorbed much talk about an artistic and poetic movement known as Symbolism. By 1890, he was attending the famous Tuesday evening literary salons hosted by Stéphane Mallarmé, the leader of the Symbolists. There he mingled with other up-and-coming writers, musicians, and intellectuals. Wagner was often the topic of conversation. Mallarmé's best-known poem, *L'Après-midi d'un faune* (*The Afternoon of a Faun*), formed the inspiration of the Debussy composition.

His relationship with Madam Vasnier, meanwhile, had become a thing of the past. It had apparently ended not long after his return to Paris. By 1890, he had met Gabrielle Dupont, the "green-eyed Gaby," and in 1891 he decided to leave his parents' home in order to move in with her. During their seven-year relationship, they lived together in Paris on rue de Londres (1891) and later on rue Gustave Doré (1893–1898).

All in all, the seven-year period that began after Debussy's return from Rome was a fruitful time in his life, and of crucial consequence. It generated many important compositions, and collaborations with other writers and artists, and helped to forge his overall aesthetics—all of which will be explored further in the following chapters of this book. But living a bohemian existence had to have been challenging. For one thing, it appears that Debussy had no steady income. To earn some money, he found work as an accompanist. He also relied on affluent patrons and financially secure friends, like the composer Ernest Chausson, whom he had met in March 1887.

It is conceivable that he found himself to be floundering outside the academy, which had given his life so much purpose and direction. While he had reached the very top of the academic hierarchy, after returning to Paris in 1887 he must have realized that he had to get back on track and keep making progress in his career. He could not afford to flounder. He needed to start his career as a professional composer, which meant he had to get his music performed and promoted.

One solution, which he found less than one year after returning from Rome, was to enter the Société nationale de musique (National Society of Music), a most serious and rarified music organization.

DEBUSSY AT THE NATIONAL SOCIETY OF MUSIC

On the surface, becoming a member of the National Society of Music was an odd choice for a wayward rebel like Debussy. The organization began in 1871, shortly after the Franco-Prussian War, when France suffered a particularly crushing and humiliating defeat to Germany. It had to cede almost all of its treasured territory of Alsace-Lorraine to Germany as well as pay an indemnity of five billion francs.

At that time, many French composers deeply resented other German threats to their identity: the overwhelming popularity of Richard Wagner's operas in French opera houses and German instrumental music in French concert halls. They felt they had to create their own platforms so that their voices could be heard. Thus the National Society of Music, with its motto "Ars Gallica," was formed at its outset as a nationalistic organization that encouraged the performance of new works by French composers. No works by foreign composers were permitted on its programs, and preference was given to absolute or abstract music genres, such as the traditional string quartet, which did not draw on extramusical sources, such as a poem or painting, for inspiration. For French composers, this kind of music was more "pure" and serious. Indeed, the original goal of the society, as written by its first secretary, Alexis de Castillon, was "to further the production and diffusion of all serious music, published or unpublished, by French composers, and to encourage and bring to light, so far as lies in its power, all musical experiments, whatever their form may be, on the condition that they reveal high artistic aspirations on the part of the composer."

Even after the society began to relax its original policy in 1886 by allowing performances of works by foreign composers, it remained a nationalist French music organization and a valuable resource for young aspiring composers like Debussy. He may have been a rebel, shocking his teachers, judges, and colleagues with his unusual harmonies and forms, but he was thoroughly French. He was one of them, and they supported him.

Debussy's role within the society was hardly as extensive as Vincent d'Indy, Ernest Chausson, and the other men who actually directed the organization; however, he was involved with it in various capacities throughout his professional life. First and foremost, he contributed nineteen new works, that is, Debussy works that had their premiere under the auspices of the national society. (This number is considerable as it constitutes approximately a third of the total number of works published during his lifetime.) The first works performed there were two of the six *Ariettes oubliées* in 1889, with the composer himself accompanying the singer Maurice Bagès on piano. The last Debussy works that were first heard in public at the National Society of Music were two of the *Douze Etudes* in November 1917, just months before his death in 1918. Other now-famous works by Debussy given their first hearing at the society include the *Prélude à "L'Après-midi d'un faune,"* the *Estampes*, *L'isle joyeuse*, the prelude "La fille aux cheveux de lin," and his orchestration of the first and third movements of Erik Satie's *Gymnopédies*.

Debussy also distinguished himself at the society as a pianist. In addition to performing a few of his own works, he played new works by other composers, such as an arrangement of Rimski-Korsakov's *Capriccio espagnol* in 1894 with composer René Chansarel. Debussy even became a member of the society's organizing committee for four different concert seasons: 1893–1894, 1897–1898, 1900–1901, and 1902. The extent of his involvement as a committee member, however, has yet to be determined and assessed.

AND NOW FOR SOMETHING COMPLETELY DIFFERENT: A STRING QUARTET

From the perspective of today, "Clair de Lune" is Debussy's most famous composition, but it was not his first masterpiece. That distinction goes to his first string quartet ("Premier quatuor en sol op. 10") of 1893, a chamber work completed just three years after the start of "Clair de Lune," yet one that sounds completely different. It seems likely that his decision to compose a string quartet in the first place was motivated by his membership in the Société nationale, which as mentioned above, favored the composition of new string quartets in the Beethoven tradition.

Outwardly, this piece loosely conforms to the traditional string quartet genre that had been established earlier by Haydn, Beethoven, and others during the classical era of Western art music. The connections between the Debussy and classical string quartet writing include the following:

1. The instrumentation of two violins, one viola, and one cello
2. A large-scale four-movement plan. The outer movements are fast while the inner movements consist of a slow movement and a dance of some sort (such as a minuet or a scherzo).
3. A first movement that uses sonata form, having an exposition (where the main themes are introduced), the development (where portions of the themes are varied and elaborated), and a recapitulation (where the main themes return)
4. Cyclicity, which means that musical material in one movement returns in one or more movements. Like the famous short-short-

short-long motive of Beethoven's Fifth Symphony, the opening theme of the Debussy quartet is the glue that binds all four movements together.

5. The name of the key as well as an opus number in the title

These and other connections between Debussy and the past, however, are not the most striking aspects of his string quartet. What makes it impossible to ignore are the groundbreaking textures, rhythms, and instrumental effects. Consider the justly famous—or infamous—scherzo movement, which is characterized by the extensive use of pizzicato, or plucking of the strings, in multiple parts. This effect, at least in the history of the string quartet genre, was novel and unprecedented, and it disturbed and displeased some members of the audience who attended the December 1893 premiere of the work by the Société nationale. Other listeners there applauded Debussy's innovation; later composers, such as Ravel, Bartók, and Ligeti, were to use pervasive pizzicato in the scherzo movements of their own string quartets. It is possible, though, that the whole idea came from the pizzicato ostinato scherzo movement of Tchaikovsky's Symphony no. 4 (1877–1878), a piece Debussy knew well. He had played it in a piano duet arrangement with Madame von Meck. Thus, the original source of the idea may very well be Tchaikovsky rather than Debussy.

The pizzicato passages in the second movement are usually regarded as the most remarkable feature of the entire quartet, but there are others worth noting. None of them, either individually or in combination, are associated with earlier string quartet music of Western Europe. Instead, they connect more directly to the music of other countries, notably Russia, Spain, and Java:

1. The brisk, widely spaced chords that open the movement evoke the strumming of a Spanish guitar.
2. The 3–2 cross-rhythms (or cross-beats) also typify Spanish-based music. In this movement, the notated meter is 6/8, which normally indicates that the six eighth notes are to be evenly divided into two groups of three. But Debussy freely adds groups of two notes instead of the expected three. The rhythmic feel of three against two is also very prominent in Spanish and Spanish-based music, such as the habanera, flamenco, and tango.

3. Still other features from the Spanish music tradition can be discerned in the Debussy, such as his use of the Spanish Phrygian scale, which sounds like a conventional minor scale with a flattened second note, and the way he alternates the Spanish Phrygian scale with other scales. The mixture of major and minor scales is another marker of flamenco music.

4. The main melody of the second movement, a faster version of the opening theme of the preceding movement, is now treated as an ostinato (i.e., the melody is repeated over and over again). In this regard, Debussy may have gone back to the pizzicato ostinato movement of Tchaikovsky's Symphony no. 4 for inspiration. As well, he might have been inspired by Javanese music, which is comprised of obvious repeated patterns.

Regardless of the sources, Debussy's string quartet must have been an otherworldly experience to the members of the Société nationale in 1893. Refreshing, if not baffling. Bold, but masterful. In effect, he had taken the classical string quartet of Beethoven, so highly esteemed by the organization, and transformed it into something uniquely his own. Technically speaking, he did so by integrating certain traits of exotic music with the more traditional compositional elements and techniques he had learned so well at the Conservatoire. In a sense, the strange result that was his string quartet was representative of the composer himself. As a successful, albeit rebellious, product of the Conservatoire system and as an active member of the serious and lofty Société nationale de musique, Debussy was a consummate insider. Yet given his family background and bohemian existence, he was also an outsider looking in. Thus, he may have had a natural affinity for exploring the music of other cultures that were outside the Western European classical repertory.

As mentioned above, not everyone attending the premiere was pleased with Debussy's quartet, but it was subsequently performed at four other Société nationale concerts. (A program survey shows that the quartet was performed in 1895, 1897, 1898, and 1912.) No other composition by Debussy appeared as frequently on the concert programs of the Société nationale.

He never wrote another string quartet. True, he said he would, and it appears that he even tried to write it. Evidence for this statement comes from a letter he wrote on February 5, 1894, to his friend Ernest Chausson, the original dedicatee of the quartet. In his October 23, 1893, letter to Chausson, Debussy wrote: "It will always be a pleasure for me to see your name attached to it [quartet]. It represents for me the beginning of a friendship which, in time, is due to become the best and most profound of my life" (*Letters*, 59). Apparently, Chausson disliked the quartet that Debussy had written expressly for him: "I should also say that I was really upset for several days by what you said about my quartet, as I felt after all it only increased your partiality for certain things which I would rather it encouraged you to forget. Anyway I'll write another one which will be for you, in all seriousness for you, and I'll try to bring some nobility to my forms."

Further evidence comes from a report by Octave Maus, a Belgian art critic who was an immediate admirer of Debussy's string quartet, calling it "the architecture of a master who is sure of his writing." In his report, which appeared in an early 1894 issue of the Belgian journal *L'Art moderne*, Maus stated that Debussy was indeed working on a new string quartet and that the third movement was completed. However, no trace of the second quartet has been found. The "premier quatuor" turned out to be Debussy's only quartet and also the only work to which he assigned an opus number. By this time, he was busy finishing a new work that would also have its premiere for the Société nationale, *Prelude to "The Afternoon of a Faun,"* one that would be even more revelatory to the listener and one would bring him much greater fame.

CONCLUSION

Because "Clair de Lune" and the String Quartet sound so different in terms of style, one might think that the young Debussy in the early 1890s was still experimenting with a range of compositional techniques and sonorities, that he had yet to hit upon a signature style. After all, his "Clair de Lune" sounds fluid and nonassertive, a suspension of time—it is the perfect background music. In comparison, the four-movement String Quartet sounds more substantial, ambitious, assertive, and decisive. (Go ahead and try to use the scherzo movement as background music, which I did at my wedding reception. The result: many guests stopped talking and stared at the musicians. It is not unobtrusive background music—it is riveting.)

In truth, neither "Clair de Lune" nor the String Quartet defines Debussy. They are just two of the pieces that comprise an already-mixed repertoire. Such diversity may connect to his lifelong concern for artistic originality and freedom. In his pursuit for the new and unusual, he refused to duplicate compositional and formal processes in his own music. A decade later, shortly after the spectacular success of his opera *Pelléas et Mélisande*, he revealed his authentic self in his September 12, 1903, letter to a friend, the composer and conductor André Messager: "Those people who are kind enough to expect me never to abandon the style of *Pelléas* are well and truly sticking their finger in their eye. Obviously they don't know that, if that were to happen, I'd turn instantly to growing pineapples in my bedroom, believing as I do that to repeat yourself is the most tiresome thing of all" (*Letters*, 141–42).

There are, however, certain threads and compositional practices that have been identified in this chapter that will run throughout his total output: unusual scales, fluctuating patterns, ambiguous harmonies, a single theme that changes and transforms throughout the course of a work, a predilection for mystery and beauty, and the habit of borrowing from other composers. Light textures and nonpulse rhythms will also be hallmarks of his life's work. This combination of traits can be better understood in the context of a late nineteenth-century literary movement in France called Symbolism, which is a subject of the next chapter.

2

IMPRESSIONIST VERSUS SYMBOLIST

Debussy thrived on change. Throughout his career, he demonstrated that he wanted to explore and grow, to take things in new directions. Such works as the *Prelude to "The Afternoon of a Faun,"* the focal work of this chapter, represent distinct breaks with nineteenth-century forms. For the conductor Pierre Boulez, it was this piece that launched the beginning of modern music. In his *Stocktakings from an Apprenticeship*, Boulez wrote:

> It has been said often: the flute of the Faune brought new breath to the art of music; what was overthrown was not so much the art of development as the very concept of form itself, here freed from the impersonal constraints of the schema, giving wings to a supple, mobile expressiveness, demanding a technique of perfect instantaneous adequacy—The potential of youth possessed by that score defies exhaustion and decrepitude; and just as modern poetry surely took root in certain of Baudelaire's poems, so one is justified in saying that modern music was awakened by *L'après-midi d'un faune*.

Debussy's concern for artistic independence in his music is analogous to the isolated position he held in France during his lifetime. He never espoused a single school of thought, and he was dismayed to find other composers imitating his own personal style. As he stated quite plainly in an interview with an Austrian journalist in 1910, "There is no Debussy school. I have no disciples; I am myself" (*DOM*, 243).

Despite Debussy's position as a revolutionary and iconoclast, it is no secret that much of what appears to be striking in his music can be associated with the ideas of artists, writers, and poets. This chapter will demonstrate how aspects of *Prelude to "The Afternoon of a Faun"* and other works have certain affinities with the literary movement known as Symbolism. Before proceeding, however, it is necessary to address his so-called connection with another movement in France, one that has stuck to Debussy like glue.

DEBUSSY THE IMPRESSIONIST: WHY AND WHY NOT

As mentioned in the preceding chapter, the first time that the word "Impressionism" was associated with Debussy was in 1887, and it was used in a negative sense. That year, Henri Delaborde, the secretary of the Académie des Beaux-Arts, officially denounced *Printemps*, one of Debussy's envois from Rome, as vague "Impressionism" because it was "one of the most dangerous enemies of truth in works of art." As evidence, Delaborde cited the emphasis that Debussy gave to "musical color" over "precision of design and form." Delaborde's choice of words here does align with common perceptions of Impressionist art. Some Impressionist painters, such as Claude Monet and Pierre-Auguste Renoir, focused on light and atmosphere over line and form. They also painted with strong bright colors and in dabs and dots, prompting critics to view their artworks as mere impressions rather than as finished products.

Delaborde's assessment was understandable as well as an uncanny prediction of Debussy's later style. Some of Debussy's music is indeed light and airy, with notes moving quickly in a soft range and resulting in a shimmering effect. His music also gives precedence to unusual sounds and timbres rather than to clearly defined themes and forms. We have already seen a representative example of this type of Debussy's music, the pizzicato scherzo movement of his String Quartet. Recall the brisk points of sound produced by the pizzicato strings in the work, which vie with the main theme for our attention.

Delaborde's assessment could also be viewed as a reflection of his own artistic preferences and style. Before becoming an art critic, he was a practicing artist who produced historical genre paintings of a conventional and realistic type, one that gave priority to firm line, precise drawing, and a highly finished surface. Thus, to an artist steeped in the classical tradition, it is understandable why he applied the term "Impressionism" to Debussy's *Printemps* as an admonishment. The fact that Debussy only submitted an unfinished score might have provided further ammunition to Delaborde that he was reviewing a musical counterpart of Impressionism in art, which he inherently disliked.

On a side note, Debussy gave what sounds like a lame excuse for submitting only a partially orchestrated version of *Printemps* to the board of the Académie. He claimed that the complete orchestral score was lost in a fire. Eventually, he did return to *Printemps*. Later versions during his lifetime include an arrangement for piano (four hands) and chorus in 1904, and an arrangement for orchestra and piano (four hands) by Henri Büsser, but with Debussy's supervision, published in 1913.

Since Delaborde, Debussy's music has been regularly classified as the musical manifestation of the Impressionist movement in painting. Just open a standard textbook on Western music history today and turn to the section on Debussy. Or read the program notes for a concert performance of a Debussy piece. Chances are you will find the term "Impressionism" applied to his music. True, some writers will note that the composer himself did not like the term. They are correct, but they will go ahead anyway and draw connections between his music and visual Impressionism. With respect to "Clair de Lune," for instance, writers have noted the incomplete chords and other ambiguous sonorities, the resonating bass notes that contribute to a sense of space and relaxation, the vague meter, and an *en plein air* depiction of a Paris evening—these and other aspects of the piece they say can be likened to the spiritual and luminous landscapes of Claude Monet.

Why does the label of Impressionism persist? One reason is because we are drawn to Debussy's unique music and want to make immediate sense of it. Labels such as Impressionism can help us to understand and distinguish his music from other kinds of "isms" in the twentieth century, such as primitivism, neoclassicism, serialism, and so on. On the flip side, the Impressionist label can hold us back from taking a closer look at Debussy's music and from considering other less obvious, but more profound, aspects of his creative work. Debussy knew this. Moreover, he thought that any label originating in other disciplines and then applied to his music was stupid, insulting, and inaccurate, and he blamed journalists for propagating such misinformation. We know his strong views on the matter because of an article he wrote in July 1901 for *La Revue blanche*, the journal that launched his career in music criticism. For this particular article, he chose to write in the form of a conversation between himself and a brutally honest character he created called Monsieur Croche (Mr. Quarter Note or Mr. Crotchet), a mouthpiece for Debussy's controversial aesthetics: "I dared to point out to him that in poetry and painting alike (and I managed to think of a couple of musicians as well) men had tried to shake off the dust of tradition, but that it only earned them the labels 'symbolist' or 'impressionist'—useful terms of abuse."

"It's only journalists doing their job who call them that," continued Monsieur Croche unflinchingly. "That's of no importance. Imbeciles can find something to ridicule in a fundamentally beautiful idea, and you can be certain there is more likely to be beauty in the work of those who have been ridiculed than in those who calmly trail along like sheep to the slaughterhouse for which they have been predestined.

"Remain unique! . . . unblemished! Being too influenced by one's milieu spoils an artist: in the end he becomes nothing but the expression of his milieu."

DEBUSSY AND SYMBOLISM

Debussy may have professed his dislike for labels, but the truth is his music leaned toward the Symbolist side of the aesthetic spectrum. This statement can be verified by a comparison of the main tenets of Symbolism and a good deal of his music, notably *Prelude to "The Afternoon of a Faun,"* his first orchestral work before the public. Following are some general principles of literary Symbolism, as shared by Paul Verlaine (1844–1896), Arthur Rimbaud (1854–1891), and Stéphane Mallarmé (1842–1898), to name just three of the leading poets here.

1. The Symbolist poets revolted against realism, specifically the realistic novel with its minute attention to detail. Gustav Flaubert's *Madame Bovary* of 1856 is often regarded as the epitome of the

realistic novel. Instead the Symbolists aimed for nuance, suggestion, and half-stated references.

2. They eschewed traditional methods of versification, such as perfect rhythmic couplets and rhythmic meters, which they regarded
   as rigid, limiting, and impersonal. Instead, they wrote poems in
   free, fluid verse and used figurative language such as metaphors,
   similes, and allegory to create vivid images. They also added double levels of meaning to their work: a surface meaning and a
   symbolic, deeper meaning.

3. In terms of subject matter, the Symbolist poets were drawn to the
   dream world, melancholy, timeless subjects, myths, mystery, and
   the supernatural. They were especially drawn to Edgar Allan Poe,
   the American writer whose own work was rich in symbolism. By
   focusing their attention inward, they believed they could avoid
   the mundane and connect more closely to emotion, the inex-
   pressible, and hidden truth.

4. They actively sought connections or "correspondences" between
   music and poetry by alliteration, assonance, and other rhetorical
   devices so that multiple senses could be engaged, resulting in a
   kind of synesthetic experience.

A good example of French Symbolist poetry is the 1876 poem *The
Afternoon of a Faun*, by Stéphane Mallarmé, the Symbolist par excellence. The poem is subtitled an eclogue, which is a pastoral dating from
the idylls of the Greek poet Theocritus (ca. 310–250 BCE). Mallarmé's
famous eclogue is about the drowsy musings of a faun, the half-human/
half-goat creature of ancient mythology and the image of Pan. According to the myth, Pan was the god of nature, shepherds, and hunters; he
is also associated with music. He is credited with the invention of panpipes, a reedless, flutelike instrument consisting of multiple cane tubes
of gradually increasing lengths. Pan fell madly in love with a beautiful
nymph named Syrinx, for whom he named his flute.

Mallarmé's poem, a long 478-word monologue, opens with the faun
waking up from a nap on a warm summer afternoon and ends with him
falling back to sleep. In between, the faun tells of his efforts to seduce
not one but two beautiful nymphs, though it is never entirely clear
whether he is describing real events, memories, or dreams.

Just by reading the first page of Mallarmé's poem, we can see that it is difficult to understand and can be subject to varied interpretations. Adding to the confusion is a profusion of images to sort through, as well as no previous context to explain what these references might be.

The Faune

These nymphs, I would perpetuate them.

So bright
Their crimson flesh that hovers there, light
In the air drowsy with dense slumbers.

Did I love a dream?

My doubt, mass of ancient night, ends extreme
In many a subtle branch, that remaining the true
Woods themselves, proves, alas, that I too
Offered myself, alone, as triumph, the false ideal of roses—

Let's see . . .

or if those women you note

Reflect your fabulous senses' desire!

One of Mallarmé's achievements in writing *The Afternoon of a Faun* was to emphasize the equivalencies between poetry and music, which reflects the general Symbolist notion of correspondences between the visible and the invisible. His intent was to combine words and images that were, like music, mysterious, ambiguous, and open to interpretation. For some interpreters, the blank spaces at the beginning and between lines of his text are comparable to the rests within and between phrases of music. For other interpreters, the blank space is the color of uncertainty.

LISTENING TO DEBUSSY'S *PRELUDE TO* *"THE AFTERNOON OF A FAUN"*

Debussy's achievement was to capture the elusive, vague, and enigmatic quality of Mallarmé's poem from a musical standpoint. He did so by composing a free interpretation of Mallarme's poem, rather than a close, line-by-line depiction. Debussy's approach makes perfect sense since the poem itself is not linear and straightforward; it is spatial, open to interpretation, and jumbled. Such qualities are entirely in keeping with a story about a confused mythical creature. The faun wakes up one summer afternoon in the forest after drinking some wine, wondering if the nymphs were real or just a vivid dream, and then falls back to sleep.

Listen now to Debussy's *Prelude to "The Afternoon of a Faun."* (Excellent recordings of the piece include those by conductors Pierre Boulez and Sir Simon Rattle.) Right from the start, the piece engages our attention with an unaccompanied flute melody, one that is played softly and calmly, symbolic of the faun playing his panpipes. There is no other sound to distract us. Contributing to the relaxing, almost sleepy, quality of the opening flute solo is the wavy shape of the melody, which slides up and down chromatically between two notes, C♯ and G. Put another way, there is no sense of forward movement, just a rocking motion. The inconsistent rhythm and vague beat also contribute to the relaxing dream world that Debussy is trying to create, as does the ambiguous key. Is the solo melody centered on C♯ or G? Or is it centered on two pitch centers? We just do not know at this point what the key of the piece is, and there are no supporting harmonies to give us a clue.

Following the flute solo, a few other instruments begin to join in. Most notably, we hear muted horn calls. (Do they symbolize hunters in the distance? Or do they convey the faun on the hunt for nymphs?) We also hear shimmering harp glissandi, perhaps a reference to the ethereal nymphs hovering in the shade of the trees. This gradual thickening of the score is telling since it nicely coincides with the faun gradually becoming more fully awake and aware of his surroundings.

The flute's sliding melody then returns for a second appearance, though varied. This time, it is accompanied by the strings, the traditional core of the classical orchestra, playing tremolos (rapid vibrations of the bow over the strings). We might expect at this point, which is approximately one minute into the piece, to have enough information to discern the key of the piece. All indications point to D major, but hold on. We have to wait a little longer, until we hear the beginning of the third statement of the chromatic flute melody before the true key of the piece, E major, emerges from the beautiful, dreamlike haze.

This concept of becoming, which is evident in the opening measures of the *Faun*, is an important factor to take into account when listening to the work in its entirety. Altogether, there are nine statements of the flute theme, with each statement a varied and longer version of the preceding one. The overall shape of the piece, however, is essentially circular and falls into three large sections. The outer sections are dominated by the flute theme and are full of indecisiveness and ambiguity. By contrast, the central section begins firmly in the key of D♭ major, an important, and relatively rare, moment of tonal clarity in the piece; has a fuller orchestration, with the strings predominating; features a more consistent and traditional four-bar phrase structure; and generally has louder dynamics.

In a sense, the overall structure is akin to a vortex, with the flute melody initially swirling inward to the center, where it recedes to the background and allows the clarinet and oboes to shine. Then the flute gradually retakes the spotlight as the music diverges outwardly, receding back to uncertainty.

Of course, the contrast between the outer and inner sections of the work is symbolic of the faun himself. He is half goat, and the flute he plays in the outer sections symbolizes the lower part of his body. He is also half man, and thus is capable of logic and reason; the solid key and full complement of strings in the central section symbolize the upper half of his body. Significantly, it is only in the more traditionally constructed central section that the faun is fully awake.

Notwithstanding Debussy's statement that his piece was a "very free illustration" of the Mallarmé poem, the circuitous design of the music is consistent with the shape of the poem. To be sure, there are many correlations between the poem and the music. For instance, the total length of the poem is 110 lines; the total length of Debussy's setting is 110 measures. A few writers have even found line-to-measure equivalencies, two of which are mentioned here:

1. Line 27 of poem reads, "Out of the twin pipes, quick to breathe." In measure 27 of the music, Debussy decides to add a second flute for the first time in the piece.
2. Line 32 of the poem reads, "Not seeing by what art there fled away together." In measure 32 of the music, Debussy uses the whole-tone scale (which lacks a central, focusing pitch) to symbolize blindness and confusion.

Still, if you were to go on an unabashed hunt for more connections between the poem and the music, you would find a large number of inconsistencies between the two works. As a demonstration, consider the proportions of the internal sections of the work. While both the poem and the music follow an overall ABA' design, Mallarmé's central B section consists of just twenty lines (42 to 61), a relatively small component of the entire 110-line poem. In contrast, the middle section of the Debussy spans forty-two measures (37–78) and is the biggest section of his piece. Possibly the best approach to take when considering the parallels between the music and the poem is that they do indeed exist and that many others can be discovered. In fact, the more often we listen to Debussy's music, the more aware we become of the almost infinite depth and intricacy beneath the smooth surface of his great music. We grasp more fully the rich complexity of his art, and why so many different interpretations of his music can exist, even side by side. One interpretation, no matter how illuminating, does not necessarily cancel out a different one.

THE BACKSTORY AND PREMIERE OF *PRÉLUDE À "L'APRÈS-MIDI D'UN FAUNE"*

Debussy began to set Mallarmé's poem to music in 1892, the same year he initiated the String Quartet. The original title of the composition was *Prélude, interlude et paraphrase finale sur l'après-midi d'un faune*, which suggests that Debussy once had a grander conception of the work. No evidence of a three-movement version exists, however, just the one-movement prelude.

He completed the full score in 1894, and the premiere performance took place at the Salle d'Harcourt in Paris on December 23, 1894, under the auspices of the Société nationale. In the days and hours leading up to the premiere, Debussy never stopped working on the score and making modifications. In his 1942 memoir *Temps et Contretemps*, the conductor Gustave Doret recalled that when he first saw the score, it was covered with Debussy's corrections. Right up to the first public performance, Debussy constantly made more corrections, honing his work of art to perfection:

> We tried; we started over; then we compared. Everyone kept calm: patience should be the watchword without which no good work can be accomplished. The piece had reached its definite form. The players, having gotten used to this new style, understood that we would have to fight a serious battle. Of course, Debussy was not unknown to the true connoisseurs, but the big public was still ignorant of him. Would it try to resist? We wondered all the more since, for this first concert, I had arranged that the hall be full and that the work not be played only for the usual limited circle of the Société Nationale.
>
> Debussy had written his masterpiece; the players and I had satisfied him, translating his thought, he said, as he had never hoped; "to perfection" he kept exclaiming at the last rehearsal.

As it turned out, the premiere performance was not perfect. In a letter to Debussy dated December 23, 1894, the writer Pierre Louÿs wrote, "To hear your piece again I shall wait for a slightly better performance. The horns stank and the rest of the orchestra was hardly better." Similarly, another Debussy friend, the composer Charles Koechlin, noted that the orchestra had insufficient rehearsal time, and that the acoustics of the Salle d'Harcourt were just not good. Nonetheless, the audience as a whole was greatly impressed because they insisted that the work be immediately repeated. Despite an in-house rule prohibiting encores, Doret and his orchestra happily broke the rule and gave a repeat performance.

Many years later, Debussy recalled that Mallarmé himself was immediately impressed. In a March 25, 1910, letter to the music critic Georges Jean-Aubry, Debussy stated that he had invited the poet to hear the piano version, to which Mallarmé responded after a long silence, "I wasn't expecting anything like that! That music prolongs the emotion of my poem and conjures up the scenery more vividly than any color" (*Letters*, 218). Mallarmé was even more impressed after hearing the work with full orchestra. In his biography of Debussy, the pianist Maurice Dumesnil states that Mallarmé had written a brief letter to Debussy following the premiere: "I have just come out of the concert, deeply moved. The marvel! Your illustration of 'The Afternoon of a Faun,' which presents a dissonance with my text only by going much further, really, into nostalgia and into light, with finesse, with sensuality, with richness. I press your hand admiringly, Debussy. Yours, Mallarmé."

SUCCESS AND CRITICISM

Relatively quickly, the *Prelude to "The Afternoon of a Faun"* became one of Debussy's most famous works. By 1906, it had been heard as far abroad as Boston (1902), Berlin (1903), Saint Petersburg and London (1904), Vienna and New York (1905), and Chicago (1906). Contemporary reviews were mixed. Following an 1895 performance of the *Prélude* in Paris, *Le Ménestrel* described the piece as "finely and delicately orchestrated; but one seeks in vain any heart or any strength. It is precious, subtle and indefinite in the same way as the work of M. Mallarmé." The *Musical Courier* of New York described it as a "curious fantasy, full of unprecise harmonies and fleeting phrases."

Both of these reviews seem to be circling around some of the same traits that we saw earlier in connection with "Clair de Lune": the light texture, fluid movement, subtlety, and the ambiguous harmonies. While some critics, over time, became more accustomed to hearing and appreciating these qualities of Debussy's, their initial reaction upon hearing the *Prélude* was one ambivalence and confusion. His style of music was too new and just not done in classical music circles. Other critics would never accept Debussy. The composer Camille Saint-Saëns, for instance, was one of Debussy's biggest detractors. His overall negative assessment of the *Prélude*, which appeared in 1920 (and thus two years after Debussy's death), suggests that the work is half-baked. As quoted by Edward Lockspeiser in *Debussy: His Life and Mind*,

> The *Prélude à l'aprés-midi d'un faune* is pretty sound, but you find in it not the slightest musical idea properly speaking. It is as much like a

piece of music as the palette a painter has worked with is like a painting. . . .

Debussy has not created a style: he cultivated the absence of style, of logic, and of common sense.

But he had a euphonious name. If he had been called Martin he would never have been talked about. In this case it is true that he would probably have adopted a pseudonym.

The last few sentences give Saint-Saëns's true motivations away: he was jealous of Debussy's greater success and achievements.

DEBUSSY THE EMANCIPATOR

Debussy's revolutionary advances encompassed the parameters of not just harmony, scale, and rhythm but also orchestration. Arguably, his supreme achievement was to transform the symphonic orchestra for he lifted the status of some instruments, such as the flute, from a supportive role to a front position. To understand his achievement in proper perspective, we need to go back in time.

In the classical symphonies of the 1780s, a midsize orchestra might have consisted of approximately forty instruments. The strings were the backbone of the orchestra. They constituted the largest section, and they were usually assigned the melody. The woodwind instruments, as a group, were smaller; they were often grouped in pairs (i.e., two flutes, two oboes, two clarinets, and two bassoons), and their role was to fill in harmony, provide body, or back up a melody. The brass section was even smaller than the woodwinds, often consisting of just two trumpets and four to six horns. As for percussion, the only instruments used were two timpani (or kettledrums). Typically, the brass and timpani appeared rarely as they were frequently reserved for the most exciting moments in a composition.

By the late nineteenth century, the size of the orchestra had swelled to an even larger size. All sections had expanded in size, and the range of percussion instruments was now fairly extensive. For the Ring cycle, Wagner's instrumentation included eight French horns (and other brass and woodwinds in groups of four, including a new instrument called the Wagner tuba), six harps, eighteen anvils, and sixty-four strings. The overall sound produced by this huge orchestra was powerful, majestic, and weighty. Because of the sheer number of instruments, there were numerous doublings of notes in Wagner's music, such as the horns doubling Wagner tubas, the trumpets in unison with trombones, and the violins with oboes and clarinets. Such instrumental padding contributed greatly to the volume and heaviness of the orchestral sound.

What Debussy did was to strip down the number of instrumental doublings at strategic moments in a work so that individual instruments could shine in a solo role. In so doing, he lightened the overall orchestral heaviness that was in vogue at the time and literally stopped the gradual expansion of the orchestra that had been going on for centuries. His decision to begin his *Prelude to "The Afternoon of a Faun,"* a one-movement orchestral work, with a solo flute melody was unprecedented, as was the subsequent interplay of other instruments in solo roles—the first harp alternating with second harp, the first horn taking turns with third horn, and so on.

This is not to say that Debussy was the first composer to begin an orchestral piece with a solo instrument. Beethoven, an earlier rebel and emancipator, inserted an improvisatory piano solo at the beginning of his Piano Concerto no. 5, known as the "Emperor Concerto," though the solo was partly accompanied by orchestra. Normally, the solo ornamental passage in a concerto (i.e., the cadenza) was reserved for the final portion of the first movement. But Debussy was the first composer to initiate a symphonic work with a solo flute, an instrument that always had a background or secondary role in an orchestral work. There was no orchestra hovering over it, nor any other instrument backing it up.

A SIGNATURE MUSICAL STYLE

As was mentioned above, there are some passages in the *Prelude to "The Afternoon of a Faun"* when the entire orchestra can be heard, notably the central B section. Listen again to a recording of the piece and focus on this section, located midway through the piece. (If you are listening to a Boulez recording, start at around five minutes in.) From this point, you will be able to hear the entire orchestra, which is rather large, performing altogether: there are three flutes, two oboes, an English horn, two clarinets, two bassoons, four horns, two harps, and a full complement of strings. Notice, too, how these full orchestra (or tutti)

passages are thick with doublings. If you are watching a live performance of the *Prélude* on YouTube, you can see the violin section playing the same melody together and bowing the same way. All that is
missing in this middle section are the two delicate crotales, or ancient
cymbals, which Debussy reserved for the last (A') section and which
contribute to the ancient, timeless quality of the work.

Thus it would not be accurate to say that the texture of *Prelude to
"The Afternoon of a Faun"* is consistently light and airy. Rather, Debussy designed the work so that the most transparent passages coincide
with the first presentation of a melody and a heavier texture with the
reiteration of a melody or the innermost sections of a work. I have
detected this light-heavy pattern in other Debussy pieces, notably the
Fantaisie for piano and orchestra. The first movement of this composition was one of the subjects of my doctoral dissertation on Debussy,
which entailed overseas research, primarily in Paris. I also studied at the
Royaumont Abbey, which is located in Asnières-sur-Oise, in the direction of Chantilly. This thirteenth-century building houses the François
Lang Library, which contains many rare music manuscripts, including
two sets of proofs of the engraved but unpublished 1890 edition of the
Fantaisie.

Every day for approximately one month, I traveled thirty miles north
from Paris to Royaumont in order to view the proofs, which contain
corrections and changes that Debussy had made by hand. Essentially, I
compared one set of proofs, dating from 1890, to a second set of proofs,
dating from 1895. My goal was to understand more fully why Debussy
made changes to the movement in the first place, what he felt the
problems were, and how he tried to fix them.

What I determined was that the 1890 version was uniformly heavy.
The first theme of the movement, for instance, had two presentations of
nearly equal weight. Debussy later tried to alleviate this uniformity by
recasting the first hearing of the opening theme as a solo and giving
more weight to the second and third restatements of the theme by
adding more instruments to double the melody. He treated the other
two themes in the movement the same way: he set their first hearings as
solos and gave more weight to the second hearings.

In sharing my research on Debussy's *Fantaisie*, I hope the reader
might see how the distinctive orchestration of his *Prelude to "The Afternoon of a Faun"* was not a one-off. He would apply this light-heavy

pattern—which is essentially a large-scale, built-in crescendo—to many other orchestral works as well, so much so that it could be considered one of his musical signatures. He transferred the pattern to other, non-orchestral settings as well, such as the opening section of "Clair de Lune" for piano, and the beginning of the beautiful second movement of the Sonata for Flute, Viola, and Harp of 1915, one of his last completed works. As you listen to other works by Debussy, chances are you will come across this distinctive hallmark of his compositional style again and again.

SUMMARY

Debussy's music is most often categorized as Impressionist or Symbolist, but he himself dismissed these terms. He shunned labels and did not want to be pinned down. Furthermore, he dismissed those critics who were trying to grasp his new style of composing. Rather, he wanted to have the freedom to draw from whatever artistic or literary movement he felt necessary to produce his unique sounds and designs. For me, Debussy's fiercely independent stance brings to mind the political positions taken by some of my friends and relatives. My mother, for instance, has been a lifelong member of the Democratic Party; however, recently she has declared herself as an independent. She does not wish to be considered either a Republican or Democrat. Debussy would understand her point of view since he too was not one thing or another. He did not belong to any camp. He was independent, which is what he claimed all along.

He especially abhorred being called an Impressionist, a term he felt was insulting, as did the artist Claude Monet and composer Maurice Ravel. Debussy did invoke the term occasionally as a way of goading Ravel, calling him "that Impressionist." Ravel, on his part, referred to Debussy as "that thief." It is also possible that the young Debussy disliked being associated with a movement that, by the 1890s, was somewhat dated. The first Impressionist exhibition took place in 1874; the sixth and last exhibition was in 1886.

While Impressionist art and Symbolist literature have several key differences, both shared a penchant for allusion and the avoidance of clear expression. It was this sense of indirect suggestion that Debussy borrowed and restated in musical terms in such works as *Prelude to "The Afternoon of a Faun,"* based on the poem by Stéphane Mallarmé. Throughout his life, Debussy did lean more often toward the Symbolist camp, which espoused timelessness and took the American poet Edgar Allan Poe as their figurehead. Consider that the first journal to hire Debussy as a music critic was *La Revue blanche*, often regarded as a leading Symbolist literary magazine. He set to music the poems of several prominent Symbolists, including Mallarmé, Baudelaire, and Verlaine. Debussy also spent years working on two Poe-motivated operas, *The Devil in the Belfry* (between 1902 and 1911 or 1912) and *The Fall of the House of Usher* (between 1908 and 1917). He did not live to finish them. As it turned out, his only completed opera was *Pelléas et Mélisande*, which is based on a Symbolist play by the Belgian poet Maurice Maeterlinck.

3

DEBUSSY AND WAGNER

An Uneasy Alliance

Debussy was a compulsive borrower, perhaps most frequently turning to the operas of Richard Wagner for inspiration. Initially, Debussy was an outwardly enthusiastic French Wagnerian (as evidence, consider the *Ariettes oubliées*). He even traveled at a young age to Bayreuth, Germany, to hear performances of Wagner's works in Festival Hall, which was specially constructed according to Wagner's directions. Subsequently, Debussy became disenchanted with Wagner—at least from all outward appearances—but his reliance on the German composer can still be discerned. Astute musicians such as Richard Strauss have detected connections between Debussy's *Pelléas et Mélisande* and Wagner. But in no sense is Debussy's great opera an example of "Wagner Lite." The rhythms in the Debussy are so different and quintessentially French.

Up until 1902, Debussy's development as a professional musician had followed mostly an upward trajectory. The list of significant milestones in his life includes a successful apprenticeship at the Paris Conservatoire, culminating in the Prix de Rome; his entry into the elite Société nationale, the music organization that supported his development and unusual vision; and the *Prelude to "The Afternoon of a Faun,"* which established his reputation as an orchestral composer. But his career really began to soar with the premiere of *Pelléas et Mélisande* at the Opéra-Comique on April 30, 1902, under the baton of André Messager.

As one might expect, any work by a composer as innovative and bold as Debussy would cause a stir, but the sheer amount of interest and controversy generated by *Pelléas* was unprecedented in the composer's output thus far, and arguably in his entire life. All the major newspapers and journals in France carried reviews of the new opera, including the largest dailies at the time: *Le Petit Parisien* (circulation: one million), *Le Petit Journal* (nine hundred thousand), *Le Journal* (six hundred thousand), and *Le Matin* (two hundred thousand). The critics for these largest newspapers were divided into two camps, pro and con. For instance, in his May 1, 1902, review for *Le Journal*, Catulle Mendès essentially derided Debussy's *Pelléas*, stating that he preferred to experience the play and music separately. He also reproached the composer for writing monotonous melodies. In contrast, André Corneau, the reviewer for *Le Matin*, had nothing but praise for the work:

> The music of *Pelléas et Mélisande* possesses originality so specialized that it would be strange if it would not encounter its detractors. . . . There are no arias so greatly favored. The personages on the stage avoid singing. They declaim in a sort of melodic speech, summarily notated, what they have to say, and the task of expressing and of communicating their sentiments is left entirely to the orchestra. . . .
>
> One should not conclude, however, that the score of *Pelléas et Mélisande*, in which melody, at least what one generally understands as melody, is absent, and in which the rhythm disappears in intentionally imprecise harmonic aggregations, is devoid of character or shape. From the initial prelude, the delicately poetic music is invested with an adorably remote color and leaves in the ear an evanescent echo of faraway things . . . for Debussy's music constantly floats above the realities of life. Its emotion is poetic, and its suffering is without a human outcry. The dream music never escapes the world of reverie.

Debussy's unusual treatment of melody in *Pelléas* was just one of his musical innovations that moved the critics and public alike. These innovations will be considered at a later point in this chapter. Here, more briefly, are some other, nonmusical, factors that combined to create such a furor:

1. *Provocative subject matter.* Fundamentally, Maurice Maeterlinck's story is a tale about adultery and jealousy, a royal love

triangle involving two brothers in love with the same girl. The story includes a bed scene, which was considered risqué at the time, and heavier plot elements of child abuse, rape, and murder.

2. *Attempted sabotage by the playwright.* Georgette Leblanc, Maeterlinck's mistress, had hoped to create the role of Mélisande and was under the impression that Debussy was pleased with her audition. When Maeterlinck, reading a newspaper, saw that another soprano had been cast, he was furious. In private, Maeterlinck stated that he was going to give Debussy "a drubbing to teach him what was what." At one point, he even barged into Debussy's home and challenged him to a duel. (Debussy fainted.) Publically, Maeterlinck stated that he hoped the opera would be an utter failure: "The *Pelléas* in question is a play that has become unfamiliar to me, almost an enemy; and being deprived of any control over my work, I am reduced to wish its fall to be quick and resounding." Those words appeared in his letter to *Le Figaro* on April 14, 1902, just a few weeks before the premiere. To make matters worse, the audience attending the April 28, 1902, dress rehearsal received an unofficial pamphlet that ridiculed Debussy's opera. It contributed to the laughing and joking in the audience during the performance. Some observers believe that Maeterlinck was himself the author of the pamphlet and put his friends up to the deed.

3. *Mélisande's English accent.* The soprano eventually cast in the title role of Mélisande was Mary Garden, who was born in Aberdeen, Scotland, and raised in Chicago, Illinois. Rumor was, she was the mistress of André Messager, the conductor and dedicatee of the opera. The audience at the dress rehearsal laughed—and not in a good way—when she mispronounced French words, such as for *courages* as *curages*. The phrase in question was "Je n'ai pas de courages," which the French audience heard as "I don't have any dirt stuck in drains."

The above factors, in conjunction with the groundbreaking music and many contradictory reviews, contributed greatly to the controversy surrounding the launch of Debussy's *Pelléas et Mélisande*. The near scandal prompted people to go and hear for themselves what the Parisian cognoscenti were all talking about. For the next ten years, Debussy's opera made more money than any other opera, including Bizet's *Carmen*, Gounod's *Faust*, and other audience favorites. It also prompted people to seek out and listen to other works by Debussy, such as the *Prelude to "The Afternoon of a Faun"* and "Clair de Lune." Thus began the widespread popularity and appreciation of much of Debussy's music, which continues to this day. With respect to *Pelléas*, by 1915, it had been played in Brussels, Frankfurt, New York, Lyon, Milan, Prague, Munich, Berlin, Rome, Boston, London, Chicago, Vienna, Buenos Aires, Geneva, Birmingham, and St. Petersburg. With respect to Debussy's music in general, in 2011, chief music critic Anthony Tommasini of the *New York Times* ranked Debussy as the fifth greatest composer in history.

THE STORY OF *PELLÉAS ET MÉLISANDE*

To fully enjoy Debussy's opera, it is best to become acquainted with the story, which is riveting. He himself was immediately entranced with it. Just a few months after attending the world premiere of Maeterlinck's play in Paris in May 1893, he was already working on the first draft of his opera.

This story of ill-fated lovers is set in the imaginary medieval kingdom of Allemonde (a pun on "the whole world") that is ruled by an old monarch named Arkël. He lives in a gloomy castle with his extended family. Genevieve is his daughter. Golaud, a widower, and Pelléas, a bachelor, are Genevieve's sons from different fathers. Yniold is Golaud's son. Altogether, there are four generations living together under one roof.

Act I

One day, while Golaud is hunting in the dark forest, he chances upon a young, beautiful, and mysterious princess from another land. Her name is Mélisande, and she is crying beside a well. Golaud brings her back home, where he introduces her to various members of his family. They marry against Arkël's wishes.

Act 2

On a hot and sunny day, Golaud's brother, Pelléas, invites Mélisande for a walk in a shady garden. They stop by a well, where the now-playful Mélisande tosses her wedding ring up in the air, only to accidentally drop it into the well water. Later, when Golaud notices that her ring is missing, he demands to know what happened. Mélisande answers with a lie, saying that she lost the ring in a cave by the sea.

Act 3

A few nights later, Pelléas comes to see Mélisande. He stands beneath her tower window, where she is combing her long and beautiful hair. During this famous scene, Pelléas asks Mélisande to lean out and let down her long, long, Rapunzel-like hair so that he can wrap himself up in it. Golaud discovers them and proceeds to scold them for behaving like children. He then leads Pelléas down to the dark and dank basement of the castle, the stench of death and decay in air. Golaud warns Pelléas to stay away from his wife. He also tells Pelléas that she is pregnant. In the final scene, Golaud questions his young son Yniold about Pelléas and Mélisande. Yniold's incomplete answers exasperate him, and Golaud squeezes his son's arm so tightly the child cries.

Act 4

Pelléas decides to leave the castle. In a castle room, he makes arrangements to meet with Mélisande one last time by the well where she had lost her wedding ring. Finding them together yet again, Golaud is enraged and beats his wife. He grabs her by her hair, drags her around the room, and throws her to the ground. Later, by the well, Pelléas and Mélisande profess their love for each other, embrace, and kiss—all the while Golaud is spying on them from behind a tree. He rushes out from his hiding place and slays his half brother with a sword. Mélisande is also wounded.

Act 5

In a bedroom in the castle, Mélisande is on her deathbed, where she has just given birth to a daughter. Golaud is both grief-stricken and guilt-ridden for murdering his brother and begs her to tell him the truth: did she commit adultery? Mélisande dies without answering him.

Maeterlinck and *The Game of Thrones?*

In a sense, Maeterlinck's play has an interesting *Game of Thrones* dynamic taking place. The lead characters are noble and dysfunctional families living in a pseudo-medieval and mythical world. There are romantic entanglements, domestic violence, and plenty of lies and castle intrigue. Scenes set in dark underground rooms contrast with scenes set outdoors in the bright sunlight. *Game of Thrones*, which is based on a series of books by George R. R. Martin called *Fire and Ice*, even has a main character called Melisandre, who is known as the Red Priestess of the Lord of Light. Like Mélisande in Maeterlinck's play (and Debussy's opera), Melisandre has long hair and a mysterious past of which we know very little. Given this shared combination of unusual traits, it is tempting to speculate that Martin might have been inspired by Maeterlinck's play or Debussy's opera; however, no firm evidence to support this conjecture exists.

It would not be wise to stretch the similarities between Martin and Maeterlinck's respective stories too far. There are plenty of differences too. On the one hand, *Game of Thrones* is a saga about seven noble families vying for power. Their ongoing fights for the Iron Throne and control of the mythical land of Westeros are among the bloodiest on television today. In *Pelléas et Mélisande*, on the other hand, the brutality is there, but the essence of the play is Symbolism. Like some other Symbolist writers, Maeterlinck carefully used words—and silence—to communicate the unexpressed and to evoke emotions. In so doing, he hoped to go beneath the mundane surface and reach the subconscious and an inner drama. To that end, he avoided literal description and careful explanations. Instead, he offered half-formed dialogue, metaphors, images, and short, repetitive phrases. Often, too, he would juxtapose seemingly unrelated ideas. A sample of his writing style will be presented shortly.

More likely, Maeterlinck and Martin each drew inspiration from earlier sources. Here are a few examples:

- Princess Bellisant, a character in *Valentine and Orson*, one of Walter Crane's "toy books." Published in London in 1870, this children's story is based on a French romance dating from the time of King Pepin (714–678 CE), the father of Charlemagne. In Crane's illustrations, Princess Bellisant has long, blond hair, and she is identified as the sister of King Pepin.
- Melisende, the Armenian Queen of Jerusalem from 1131 to 1153. She is slender, has dark hair, and is known as the Crusader Queen. Her name resurfaces in Miguel de Cervantes's *Don Quixote* (1605). Like Princess Bellisant, however, she is described here as a noble woman with fair hair. For Cervantes, Melisende is a daughter of Charlemagne.
- Melusine, the daughter of a medieval king who usually lives in a forest. Every Saturday she becomes a mermaid with twin tails. Her story also dates to medieval times. The most translated version is the *Chronique de Melusine* (1393) by Jean D'Arras.

In the end, we cannot pinpoint with any degree of certainty which version of the legend inspire Maeterlinck and Martin. One thing is for sure: the legend of Mélisande is very old and has undergone various transformations throughout history. Most often, she is described as an aristocrat with long, blond hair. The forest and a castle are common settings of her story. Surely, the version that resonates most often today is Melusine, the two-tailed mermaid who has resurfaced (!) in the Starbucks logo. She is also a character in the video game series *Final Fantasy*.

A SAMPLE OF MAETERLINCK'S LANGUAGE

The following passage will serve as a demonstration of the mysterious quality of Maeterlinck's text, which some of his detractors considered to be inarticulate but which Debussy so admired. This is the passage where Golaud, lost in the forest, meets Mélisande, another lost and wandering character:

GOLAUD. No matter how I try, I can't find my way out of this forest—God knows where this wild boar has led me. I thought I'd wounded it and it would die there and then. There's its blood. But now I don't know where it can have got to. I don't know where I am myself. Even my hounds have lost track of me. I'll retrace my steps. Perhaps . . . Is that . . . Someone weeping? Oh! Who can that be by the edge of the water? Sobbing her heart out! There, by the fountain? (*He coughs*) She hasn't heard. I can't make out her face. (*He comes near and touches Mélisande on the shoulder.*)

GOLAUD. Why are you crying?

MELISANDE. Don't touch me! Don't touch me!

GOLAUD. Don't be afraid. I wouldn't do you any . . . Oh! How beautiful you are.

MELISANDE. Don't touch me or I'll throw myself in the water.

GOLAUD. I'm not going to touch you. Look, I'll stay here by the tree. Don't be afraid. Has someone hurt you?

MELISANDE. Yes! Yes! Yes! Yes! (*She sobs loudly.*)

GOLAUD. Who is it has hurt you?

MELISANDE. They all have! Everyone!

GOLAUD. How have they hurt you?

MELISANDE. I don't want to talk about it! I can't talk about it . . .

GOLAUD. Come! Don't cry like that. Where are you from?

MELISANDE. I'm running away. Away from . . .

GOLAUD. Yes. Yes. Where are you running away from . . . ?

MELISANDE. I'm lost . . . lost here . . . I don't come from here . . . I wasn't born there . . .

GOLAUD. Where are you from? Where were you born then?

MELISANDE. Oh! Oh! Far away. Far . . . far . . .

GOLAUD. What's that gleaming in the depths of the water?

MELISANDE. Where? . . . oh, that is the crown he gave me. It fell off while I was crying.

GOLAUD. A crown! Who is it crowned you? I'll try to get it back.

MELISANDE. No, no. I don't want it any more! I'd rather die here and now . . .

GOLAUD. I can easily get it back. The water isn't that deep.

MELISANDE. I don't want it anymore. If you try to get it back I'll jump in myself instead.

GOLAUD. No. Never mind. I'll leave it where it is. It looks very beautiful. Is it long since you ran away?

MELISANDE. Yes . . . yes. Who are you?

GOLAUD. I am the prince Golaud. Grandson of King Arkël, the old king of Allemonde.

The above passage can be understood in more than one way, but it seems that Maeterlinck is repeatedly juxtaposing a certain kind of duality: clarity and mystery. Golaud is the one who comes across as an open book. He does not hesitate to say what he thinks and who he is: "Oh! How beautiful you are," and "I am the prince Golaud." He tries to get as much information as he can out of Mélisande by asking her a series of probing questions. In fact, just about every time he speaks, he asks a question. He wants clarity.

Mélisande, by contrast, is a study in obscurity. We really do not know who she is or where she comes from. It can be inferred that she is an aristocrat since she lost her crown and that she is a long way from home. It is possible that she is a victim of abuse. She is crying and cowering. She repeats herself and leaves sentences unfinished, as if she is dazed. She cannot or will not explain herself very well, only infrequently responding to Golaud's barrage of questions. It is as if she is traumatized and numb. Both Pelléas and Mélisande do have at least one thing in common, though: they are both lost souls in the forest.

Given Mélisande's strange and exotic persona, the decision to cast Mary Garden in the title role of Debussy's opera was a wise one in retrospect. Her Scottish-American accent must have sounded foreign to French audiences and thus was entirely in keeping with her role as a princess from afar. The decision was not, as Maeterlinck claimed, inherently biased against him or his mistress Georgette Leblanc, who had campaigned so earnestly for the part. From all accounts, Leblanc was a strong, socially outgoing, and determined person—hardly a good fit for the waiflike Mélisande. Further, and as explained by the head of the Opéra Comique, Albert Carré, Leblanc "lacked the physical qualities of the woman-child character that was Mélisande." In his book *Souvenirs de théâtre*, he clearly indicated that the petite Mary Garden, who weighed all of ninety-eight pounds, was the perfect young woman to create the coveted role.

Full disclosure: Maeterlinck initially conceived of his Mélisande as a princess of unknown origin, which is how she is portrayed in modern performances of Debussy's opera. This was not, however, the case in 1902, when the opera was first performed. Some viewers back then knew very well who she was: one of the wives of the notorious Bluebeard, the serial wife murderer of fiction. As the legend goes, Bluebeard was an evil aristocrat who killed his six wives. Only the seventh and last wife was able to escape his castle. French operagoers in 1902 were familiar with the story of Bluebeard because of two works that had appeared in Paris just the year before: Maeterlinck's play *Ariane et Barbe-bleue* (*Ariadne and Bluebeard*) and Georges Méliès's silent film *Barbe-bleue*. In Maeterlinck's telling of the tale, the wives have names, one of whom is called Mélisande. (Yes, Maeterlinck's *Ariadne and Bluebeard* contains yet another embodiment of the medieval Melusine.)

TWO LISTENING EXCERPTS

Prelude

Listen now to the beginning of Debussy's opera. One good recording is by Herbert von Karajan conducting the Berlin Philharmonic Orchestra, from the 1970s, with Richard Stilwell and Frederica von Stade in the title roles. Another good recording and video of the entire opera can be accessed on YouTube and includes English subtitles. This is Peter Stein's production from Cardiff, with conductor Pierre Boulez. For our purposes here, just cue in to approximately the first two minutes of the video, which comprises the opening orchestral prelude.

First, listen for the three main melodic ideas or motives that are introduced in the prelude. All three are quite short but will be repeated, sequenced, or transformed later in the opera.

The first motive, which various writers have called the "Enigma of the World" or "Times Past" or simply "the Forest," occurs in the opening four measures of the opera. It consists of slow-moving notes sounding in a low, deep register and gives the impression of a stately procession. This is fitting music for a dark forest setting with old looming trees.

Whereas the first motive is associated with a landscape, the second connects with a character. This is Golaud's motive, which is brought forward immediately after the forest motive. It consists of just two different alternating chords. Significantly, this first presentation of Golaud's motive has an active dotted rhythm, a reflection of his energy for hunting a wild boar in the forest. The back-and-forth chords serve to undercut his quest for forward action, however. For all his intents and purposes, this hunter is not going anywhere. He is lost.

Golaud's motive gives way to a restatement of the solemn forest motive, which in turn is followed by the second hearing of his motive. This time, the dotted rhythm has been removed, suggesting a lack of direction. Golaud has gotten further lost in the forest.

Finally, there is Mélisande's motive, which is relatively easy to identify. Played initially in unison by the two oboes, her simple melody is placed in the highest register of the opera thus far. It flows along in an archlike curve, and thus is the only motive of the three to have a perceptible shape. The accompaniment meanwhile is alive with movement, with the upper strings played *sur la touche* (on the fingerboard) and *divisi*—two of Debussy's ways for thinning out the texture. Both the melody and accompaniment combine to convey Mélisande's lightness, grace, and naïveté.

Before continuing to act 1, back up and listen to the short prelude again. This time, pay special attention to how the three motives and their restatements are arranged.

You may have noticed that the first two motives, the Forest and Golaud, essentially alternate throughout the prelude, with Mélisande's motive serving as an interruption to the stiff pattern. Truly, this foreign princess is a breath of fresh air. The visual layout of the sequence of these melodic events in the prelude thus might look like this:

Forest—Golaud—Forest—Golaud—Mélisande—Golaud—Forest

Curtain rises.
Then Golaud enters.

Debussy's orchestral prelude does more than just introduce the recurring characters and ideas of Maeterlinck's play. It also encapsulates the story in broad outline and accurately predicts what is to come. For instance, at the end of Maeterlinck's play, Mélisande dies shortly after giving birth to a daughter, prompting King Arkël to state, "Now it is the poor child's turn." With these words, the tragedy of life, love, and destiny is brought full circle. Debussy discerned the essential circularity of the play and replicated it in the shape of his prelude, which begins and ends with the Forest motive. The internal sequence of events in the prelude tells us that although Mélisande will come to be a part of Golaud's life, she is only there temporarily. Moreover, he himself will never really change. He will always be lost in a forest.

One last observation about the prelude has to do with the contrasting "harmonic fields" of each of the three motives. These fields are not obvious to new listeners, but they are essential to Debussy's compositional process:

1. To give the Forest motive a timeless quality, he used Dorian mode, which dates back to ancient Greece. This mode resembles

our current natural minor scale but is distinguished by the raised sixth degree.

2. To underscore that Golaud is lost, at the beginning of the prelude Debussy selected the whole-tone scale. Unlike modern major and minor scales, the whole-tone scale lacks half steps, which provide directional tendencies. Put another way, since all the notes of this scale are equally spaced, they do not lead to any place in particular.

3. Finally, Debussy used a pentatonic scale for the tender and exotic Mélisande, no doubt because it is associated with music of non-Western cultures, like Java, as well as simple folk songs.

Act 1, Scene 1

Continue to listen and view the first scene of the opera, during which Golaud is hunting in the forest and stumbles across the beautiful Mélisande crying beside a pond. (Cue to 2:10 of the Boulez video, and watch until the 11:00 mark.)

One of the first things you might have noticed is that the base dynamic level of the scene is soft and subdued. While there are orchestral surges, they are brief rather than sustained, and they often subside into an underlying silence. For instance, when Golaud boasts that he is a prince and a grandson of King Arkël (7:30), the orchestra executes a rather tiny two-measure crescendo. The first measure of the crescendo consists of just horns, bassoons, and double basses—all entering *piano*. By the start of the second measure, these instruments have swelled to *forte* and are joined by the clarinets, oboes, and the remaining strings. The result is a built-in orchestral crescendo. Coinciding with the peak of the crescendo is the start of a *diminuendo*. By the next (third) measure of the excerpt, the horns, clarinets, and oboes have disappeared while the strings have faded to *piano* or *pianissimo*.

Such restless mini-swells and dissipations throughout the opera suggest that there are strong emotions simmering beneath the quiet surface. It is only during the love scene at the end of act 4 that emotion and passion are unleashed (2:03:20). Here, Pelléas finally declares his love to Mélisande in an "aria" that is the emotional climax of the work ("On dirait que ta voix a passé sur la mer au printemps"). He begins his declaration softly, the orchestra reduced to a gentle and polite accompanying. Gradually, the orchestra gathers strength, swelling louder and louder, and at times drowning out Pelléas, a premonition that Golaud is about to murder him.

But perhaps your first impression had more to do with the singers' often wispy, fragmentary melodies, which are so unlike typical operatic singing. You could even say that the entire first scene is just a long dialogue between Golaud and Mélisande. The truth is, neither they nor any of the other characters ever reach the point of singing an actual song, not only here but during the entire opera as well. (This may be one reason that excerpts of the opera rarely appear on solo recital programs. Another is because the singing is tied closely with the action on stage.) Nor will you ever hear other conventions associated with opera, such as long, showy arias, or the duets, trios, and other ensembles that enliven most operas. These traditional set pieces usually have clear meter, regular rhythms, and identifiable forms. By contrast, the characters in *Pelléas et Mélisande* simply sing, one after another, in a mostly syllabic style (one syllable per note), and their rhythms tend to avoid strong beats.

The melodic style of *Pelléas et Mélisande* was atypical for the time. Consider, for instance, Richard Strauss's first reaction when he heard the opera in 1907. This outstanding German composer attended the performance as a guest of the novelist Romain Rolland, whose recount of the evening is a fascinating read (see his *Richard Strauss et Romain Rolland: Correspondence, Fragments de Journal*). After hearing the first act, Strauss turned to Rolland and said, "Is it like this all the time? Nothing more? There's nothing in it. No music. It has nothing consecutive. No musical phrases. No development." When told that there were musical phrases, but these were just not stressed or underlined in a way the public could readily understand, Strauss replied, "But I am a musician and I hear nothing."

Given his vivid and highly programmatic music, which is so unlike Debussy's subtle music, Strauss's reaction is understandable. Perhaps his most recognizable composition is *Also Sprach Zarathustra*, with its magnificent opening signifying strength, vastness, and the dawn of a new age. We know it today as the theme from *2001: A Space Odyssey*.

Strauss's comments are just plain wrong. There is something in Debussy's opera, and there is music in it. We just need to shift our mindset and consider his melodic style beyond the conventional expectations of music from the common-practice period. We need to go further back to the turn of the seventeenth century, when opera began, if not to a much earlier in time, when the old Arcadian poems of ancient Greece were written. This is because the syllabic melodies with no pulse in *Pelléas et Mélisande* resemble monody, a term that describes the simple, expressive, and speechlike singing style of the first operas, which in turn were supposed to be based on the musical practices of the Greeks. The full-blown operatic display arias, designed to show off the singers' talents, came later, as did other big set pieces and scenes.

MAKING SENSE OF DEBUSSY'S OPERA

As we know, Debussy was not one for revealing his compositional craft, but given that his opera is a musical setting of one of Maeterlinck's timeless fairy tales, it seems plausible that he turned to the distant musical past for inspiration. Just as fairy-tale characters speak naturally and utter simple truths of which they themselves are unaware, so do Maeterlinck and (in turn) Debussy's characters. Stiff conventions of composition would have been out of place in their respective arts. For instance, the quicker pace generated by rhyming couplets would detract from the timeless, nebulous world both men were trying to create.

Besides viewing Debussy's opera as a fairy tale, we can make sense of it by keeping in mind a few of the compositional strategies he takes throughout his work.

Duplication

Often, when presenting a melodic idea or a recurring motive, Debussy tends to repeat it immediately, either exactly or with minimal variation. One such duplication occurs when Golaud says to himself, "I must retrace my steps." Starting at 2:56 and ending at 3:07, listen in the orchestral part for a variation of his motive, which sounds both before and after he admits he is lost. Notice, too, that the active dotted rhythm that had distinguished his motive in the prelude is altogether missing in this reiteration, subtly emphasizing that Golaud is indeed lost and is not moving forward.

Debussy employs this process of duplication frequently, not only in *Pélleas*, but in much of his other music as well. His intention might have been twofold. On the one hand, he gives listeners the chance to slow down and take in the music. On the other hand, he maintains the childlike quality of Maeterlinck's fairy tale. The duplications, both in the text and music, are analogous to repeated syllables in baby talk ("Mama" and "Dada").

Silence

Just as the duplications allow listeners to think and reflect, so do the many silences that characterize the works of both Maeterlinck and Debussy, and of many other Symbolists as well. For Maeterlinck, silence is indicated visually by the many ellipses that appear in the play. For Debussy, silence results aurally when the instruments or voice parts drop out.

With regard to the opera, silence operates on more than one level. First, it is used to signify timelessness. When the "Times Past" motive recurs in the prelude and first scene, the music sometimes disappears momentarily or is pared down to a lone instrument. In addition, silence is manipulated to bestow drama and expression. When Mélisande utters her first words in the opera ("Don't touch me. Don't touch me"), the orchestra is kept entirely silent. There is no other sound to detract our attention from the powerful emotion—in this case, fear—she is experiencing. Rather, the lack of orchestral sound intensifies the moment.

Symbolism

Look for the many skillful ways Debussy converts the Symbolist elements of Maeterlinck's play into music. Some of these elements have been mentioned above, but there are many others. Especially important is the duality of darkness and light that underpins both the play and the music. The second and third scenes in act 3 of the opera will serve as a demonstration of the opposing symbols of darkness and light (cue to 1:12:00).

Scene 2 takes place in the castle vaults at the midpoint of the opera. The vaults are located underneath the castle, which is built on a chain of caverns and includes an underground lake. Golaud intentionally leads Pelléas to the deep, dark lake as a way of warning his brother to stay away from his wife.

GOLAUD. My God! Do you not see? One more step and you would have fallen down that great hole!

PELLEAS. But I didn't see it. Not enough light from the lantern . . .

GOLAUD. My mistake . . . but if I hadn't grabbed you by arm . . . Anyway, there you are! Look. That's the stagnant water I told you about. Smell the stench of death that comes up from it. Let's go on to the end of this path with the low ceiling; and be sure to bend down a little. It could strike against your head.

PELLEAS. I smell it even now. Like the odor of a tomb.

To create mystery and terror in this scene, Debussy turned again to the whole-tone scale (although there are some extraneous notes). He also used pedal points, repeated notes, descending scalar segments, and mostly low-sounding instruments, such as bassoons and cellos, to indicate the stagnant water and death. At the moment when Golaud asked Pelléas if he can see the deep chasm, Debussy outlined the vocal melody with a tritone, an interval that has been historically associated with death.

By contrast, the following interlude and scene 3 take place in the fresh air outdoors (1:16:14), the brothers having just climbed the stairs from the vaults. Now we hear ascending intervals, fluttery flute ostinatos that bring to mind birds warbling, and harp glissandi that sound like running water. The net effect is one of vibration, motion, and light.

WAGNER IN PELLÉAS

We can also make sense of Debussy's famous opera by taking into consideration the music and aesthetics of his onetime idol, Richard Wagner. Indeed, Wagner was perhaps the main influence on Debussy's development as a composer, and there is a complex of connections among their respective works. Certain aspects of *Pelléas*, for instance, are straight out of Wagner's *Tristan und Isolde*. A married woman's love for another man and a jealous husband who murders his wife's lover are just two commonalities of plot. Debussy also adopted some of Wagner's compositional techniques. Both men used the orchestra as a commentator to the action, and sometimes their orchestras seem to be smarter than the characters. For example, when Golaud asks Mélisande, "What's that gleaming in the depths of the water?" the orchestra is one step ahead. That is, the soft, one-beat fanfare played by the horns—right before Golaud asks his question—gives away the answer to the audience: it is a gold crown. Nearly half a century earlier, Wagner had used similar foreshadowing techniques in *Das Rheingold* and his other operas.

It is hardly surprising that Debussy was so taken was Wagner. How could he not be? After Beethoven, Wagner was the most influential composer in nineteenth-century Europe. He cast a long shadow that extended all the way through the twentieth century and beyond Europe. Consider his development of a special operatic technique called leitmotif (leading motive), which is a musical theme that recurs in an opera to represent characters, objects, ideas, and landscapes. In Wagner's hands, the leitmotif was subject to transformation, depending on context. Subsequent generations of composers took Wagner's leitmotif technique and ran with it. One of these composers was Max Steiner, who was born in Austria but eventually moved to Hollywood in 1929 to compose film music. In *Gone with the Wind* (1939), for instance, he quoted "Dixie" at the beginning of the movie in order to set the scene squarely in a happy, pre–Civil War South. At a later point in the film, when Scarlett O'Hara walked in between the injured Confederate soldiers in the Atlanta railroad station, Steiner set "Dixie" in a sad minor key, rather than the original major key. The change from major to minor is just one way that composers like Steiner could effect thematic transformation.

With respect to Debussy, his connections to Wagner were both subtle and obvious. While he clearly used thematic transformation of the leitmotiv, for example, his habit was to create brief motifs not more than four measures in length. These wispy melodies correspond perfectly to the vague and fleeting gestures in Maeterlinck's story and its elusive syntax. Debussy's technique of thematic transformation was subtle as well. He tended to alter specific intervals and rhythm instead of effecting drastic changes, such as changing the overall melodic contour. Moreover, his motifs tended to just hint at the emotions, characters, and events on stage at any one time, rather than spell them out. Wagner's leitmotifs, by contrast, could extend beyond four measures (think of the Siegfried leitmotif, for example) and were developed by the orchestra to express deep emotion and psychological progression throughout the whole opera. They tended to announce the action on stage so obviously and clearly that critics of Wagner's music called them "musical visiting cards." Debussy, too, thought Wagner's leitmotif technique was crass, a crutch for "those who are unable to follow a score."

Many obvious connections between Wagner and Debussy occur in the interludes, the orchestral passages between the scenes and acts. According to conductor André Messager, Debussy had to expand some of the interludes in *Pelléas et Mélisande* just weeks before the premiere of the opera because he failed to realize how long it would take to change scenery. As one might imagine, Debussy was in a rush; his quick solution was to default to the brilliant operas of Wagner. Since the 1902 premiere, several writers have located a treasure trove of explicit Wagnerian source material in Debussy's opera interludes, especially *Parsifal*, *Tristan und Isolde*, and *Die Meistersinger*.

One could argue that there is at least one motif in *Pelléas et Mélisande* that is overtly Wagnerian. This is Golaud's motif, which is distinguished by a dotted rhythm, a signifier of the hunter and his sword. (A similar rhythm marks the theme of Siegfried, Wagner's mythical prince who is a dragon slayer.) Compared to Mélisande's and other motifs in the opera, Golaud's is the one that is transformed the most often in the Wagnerian manner. Sometimes Debussy even has his orchestra introduce Golaud's motif in the "musical visiting card" manner or, as described above, give him a gentle nudge. By treating Golaud's motif in the old Wagnerian way, Debussy seems to reveal the view he had of this character as old, crude, not very intelligent, and discontented.

DEBUSSY AND WAGNER

As mentioned earlier in this chapter, Debussy idolized the music and aesthetics of Richard Wagner, at least during the period extending from the late 1880s and though the early 1890s. He himself would later cite 1889 as the height of his infatuation with Wagner: "I was full of the

Wagnerian madness" (*DOM*, 167). During this time period, he attended *Lohengrin* and *Tristan und Isolde* in Paris. Regarding the performance of Tristan at the Concerts Lamoureux in 1887, Debussy wrote, "Decidedly the finest thing I know." As well, like many other French composers of time, he made two pilgrimages to Bayreuth in northern Bavaria, to experience Wagner's operas in their specially designed venue. His first trip to Bayreuth was in 1888, when he heard *Parsifal* and *Die Meistersinger*. The following year he made a second trip, this time to hear *Tristan und Isolde*. To be sure, Debussy was part of a growing "cult of Wagner" in France, which included his friends Ernest Chausson and Paul Dukas as well as the Symbolist writers Baudelaire, Verlaine, and Mallarmé.

Various works of these Frenchmen employed Wagnerian themes, methods, and beliefs. For instance, the Symbolist notion of "correspondences" between the arts traces back to Wagner's concept of Gesamtkunstwerk, or total work of art, in which all the arts combine into a single work to transcend the possibilities of the individual media. In the case of Debussy, his so-called Wagnerian works feature extreme chromaticism and heavy orchestration, two of Wagner's notable characteristics. These works include the following:

- *La Damoiselle élue* (1889), a lyric cantata for soprano, female chorus, and orchestra. Though based on the poem by Dante Gabriel Rossetti, the founder of the Pre-Raphaelite Brotherhood in England, this work presents leitmotifs and multiple allusions to *Parsifal*.
- Several song collections, such as *Cinq Poèmes de Baudelaire* (1889); *Proses lyriques* (1892–1993), of which Debussy himself was the author; *Ariettes oubliées* (1886–1887) on poems by Verlaine; and *Fêtes galantes* (first series; 1891), also based on poems by Verlaine.
- The *Fantaisie* for piano and orchestra (1889–1890), a three-movement concerto that was never performed during Debussy's lifetime. He refused to allow its performance, possibly because of the heavy orchestration. He would later revise the score, in part to alleviate the heavy, uniform texture, but he never finished the project.

- *Rodrigue et Chimène*, an opera Debussy began in 1890 but never completed. The libretto was written by Catulle Mendès, an early supporter of Wagner's music in France and a contributor to the *Revue wagnérienne*.

To this collection of Wagnerian works belongs *Pelléas et Mélisande*, which was begun in 1893.

At the height of Debussy's "Wagnermania," he began to grow disillusioned. By 1893, he planned to write an article, "On the Uselessness of Wagner," although no trace of this diatribe exists. From then on, his attitude toward his former idol continued to sour. While respecting Wagner's accomplishments and genius, Debussy resented this German composer's dominance over current French music. By the time *Pelléas et Mélisande* was staged, he thought Wagner was an end rather than a beginning, whose music was a virtual compendium of mid- and late nineteenth-century musical style. In an April 1902 note entitled "Why I Wrote *Pelléas*," he stated,

> After some years of passionate pilgrimages to Bayreuth, I began to have doubts about the Wagner formula, or, rather, it seemed to me that it was of use only in the particular case of Wagner's own genius. He was a great collector of formulae, and these he assembled within a framework that appears uniquely his own only because one is not well enough acquainted with music. And without denying his genius, one could say that he put the final period after the music of his time, rather as Victor Hugo summed up all the poetry that had gone before. One should therefore try to be "post-Wagner" rather than "after Wagner."

The phrasing in the final sentence is interesting, especially the words "post-Wagner" and "after Wagner." In English, the words "post" and "after" could be understood as synonyms, but this is not so in French. The original words written by Debussy, "après" and "d'après," may be translated as "after" and "according to the opinion of." Consequently, Debussy seems to be stating that he viewed Wagner in 1902 both as the end of a period and as someone to go beyond in order to chart a new path, rather than as a model.

A few years later, he would poke fun of Wagner in "Golliwog's Cakewalk," the sixth and final movement of *Children's Corner* for solo piano

(1908). In the central section of the piece is a quotation from the beginning of Wagner's *Tristan und Isolde*. The recurrence of the soaring love-death leitmotif from a German opera about noble lovers in a ragtime-inspired piece about Golliwog, a rag doll, can only be interpreted—then and now—as a mocking gesture. Adding further to the insult is Debussy's performance marking over the quoted material, *cédez, avec grande emotion* (slower with great emotion), which focuses our attention squarely on the parody in play. You cannot miss it. He even instructed the pianist Maurice Dumesnil, one of Debussy's favorite pianists, not to be afraid to "overplay" the quotation.

CONCLUSION

In sum, Debussy's aesthetic position on Wagner music was shifting and complex. He had a true love-hate obsession with the great German composer. Musically speaking, his ties to Wagner in *Pelléas et Mélisande* were also complex. Some were overt while others were subtle. Debussy's opera, however, was uniquely different from Wagner's operas. The brief, fragmentary melodies and the varied harmonic fields that fluctuate that than drive toward resolution capture Mélisande's fragmented mind. These features are decidedly non-Wagner, as is Debussy's lighter orchestra, which neither doubles nor connects directly to the characters' melodies. Moreover, his orchestra is frequently silent—another aspect of the music that conveys detachment, an existence elsewhere. This is not to say that Debussy's opera lacks structural coherency. On the contrary, the various rhythms, melodies, and harmonic fields are arranged in circular tableaux of varying size. Such designs are quintessentially French but were directly inspired by the circular shapes within Maeterlinck's story.

At various times in his life, Debussy worked on several other opera projects, but he never finished any of them. These include the following:

- "Rodrigue and Chimène," based on a libretto by Catulle Mendès (1890–1893)
- "The Devil in the Belfry," based on the short story by Edgar Allan Poe (1902–1911)

- "The Fall of the House of Usher," after another Poe story (1908–1917)

Pelléas et Mélisande proved to be Debussy's only completed opera as well as his most esteemed work. Ironically, three other composers were drawn to Maeterlinck's drama, which they instinctively recognized as a pathway for new kinds of music. Altogether, the four *Pelléas et Mélisandes* are Claude Debussy's five-act opera (1893–1902), Gabriel Fauré's concert suite of incidental music, op. 80 (1898), Arnold Schoenberg's symphonic poem, op. 5 (1902–1903), and Jean Sibelius's concert suite of incidental music, op. 46 (1905). The most successful *Pelléas et Mélisande*? Probably the Debussy, thanks in part to the well-publicized premiere.

4

DEBUSSY AND RAVEL

Debussy's personal life until 1902 was turbulent. In the 1890s, he went through a succession of girlfriends, including an on-again/off-again relationship with Gaby Dupont, whom he had met in the spring of 1890. They lived together for several years, starting in July 1893, but he apparently left her for a soprano named Thérèse Roger in February 1894. At that time, he announced his engagement to Mlle. Roger, but he did so in order to impress his friend and generous benefactor Ernest Chausson, who disapproved of Debussy's promiscuity and association with Gaby Dupont. He wanted Debussy to settle down and live a more respectable life. Chausson soon learned that Debussy had not really severed his relationship with Gaby Dupont, that Debussy had lied to him, and that he had used Thérèse. By the middle of March 1894, scarcely one month later, the friendship between Chausson and Debussy was over, as was Debussy's engagement to Thérèse Roger.

Gaby Dupont was a main figure in Debussy's life in the years leading up to the premiere of *Pelléas et Mélisande* and worldwide fame. Despite their stormy relationship, she was one of his sources of emotional and financial support while he worked on his compositions. As to how she supported him financially, it is not clear. She has been variously described as a laundress, a washerwoman, and a milliner. Debussy once referred to her as his secretary. She later recalled that the "painful scenes" in their relationship stemmed from a lack of money. To be sure, a close friend of the composer reported that during this time Debussy did not even know where his next dinner would come from.

In February 1897, Gaby Dupont attempted suicide by shooting herself with a revolver, shortly after finding a love letter from another woman in Debussy's pocket. Gaby was not even seriously hurt, but in April of that year Debussy himself began to speak of suicide too. Their relationship was finally over by the end of 1898, and a few months later he began to see a young fashion model named Marie-Rosalie Texier, whose nickname was Lilly. Claude and Lilly were married on October 19, 1899.

It was during the late 1890s that Debussy met Maurice Ravel (1875–1937), the other composer most often associated with Impressionism. Subsequently, during the first decades of the twentieth century, they were frequently pitted against each other as rivals. Today, their names are often mentioned together, and their music understood as two sides of the style. In truth, their association was complicated, shifting over time. There are also, of course, some fundamental distinctions of style to be made, which will be considered shortly.

RAVEL'S EARLY LIFE, TRAINING, AND COMPOSITIONS

But first, some aspects of Ravel's biography: born in 1875, he was thirteen years younger than Debussy. Maurice's father Joseph was a civil engineer and inventor of Swiss origin, who liked all things mechanical. He would sometimes take his two children, Maurice and Edouard (1878–1960), to admire the machinery used in factories in Europe and abroad. Ravel would continue to visit factories as an adult. During his one and only concert tour in North America in 1928, besides conducting and performing in New York, Boston, Chicago, Toronto, Montréal, and other capital cities, he took time out from his busy schedule to visit the Ford motor plant in Detroit. The hypnotic, repetitive rhythm of *Boléro*, his most famous and enduring work, was in fact inspired by a factory assembly line.

Ravel's mother Marie, by contrast, was of Basque origin and had lived in northern Spain, where in 1872 she had met her husband Joseph Ravel. At that time, Joseph was a mining engineer and was involved in the construction of a new Spanish railroad. Their son Maurice was born in Ciboure in southwestern France, just a few miles from the Spanish border. This is the French side of Basque country. Although the Ravels moved to Paris when Maurice was three months old, he grew up hearing his mother sing Spanish folk melodies. The musical styles from his mother's Spanish and Basque origins would later inspire his own original compositions. For instance, the rhythm that is repeated incessantly throughout his *Boléro* resembles the traditional Spanish dance from which the piece takes its name. Some of his other "Spanish" works include the *Rapsodie espagnole*, an orchestral suite; and *L'Heure espagnole* (*The Spanish Hour*), an opera. He would retain a lifelong attachment to the land of his birth, returning regularly to Saint-Jean-de-Luz, a beach resort adjacent to Ciboure, for the summer holidays.

Like the young Debussy, Ravel began his formal musical studies on piano and harmony at the Paris Conservatoire. This was in 1889, when he was fourteen years old. According to his teachers, he was a gifted pianist with a spirited temperament, and he won a piano competition in 1891. Thereafter, he failed to win any other first prizes in piano performance and was dismissed in 1895. Just as Debussy turned from piano to composition following his rejection from the Conservatoire, so did Ravel. He reentered the Paris Conservatoire in 1897 to study composition with Gabriel Fauré (1845–1924) and counterpoint with André Gédalge (1845–1926).

Unlike Debussy, Ravel did not succeed nearly as well. Between 1900 and 1905, he had tried a total of five times to win the Prix de Rome, the ultimate goal of compositional training at the Paris Conservatoire, but had failed. The closest he came to winning the coveted award was third prize in 1901 for his cantata *Myrrha*. For his final attempt in 1905, he submitted two pieces:

1. A Fugue in C, which contained obvious parallel fifths, an ungainly, medieval-sounding movement considered "forbidden" in tonal music. He also ended the piece with a seventh chord, which produces an opened-ended sound. This is hardly a fitting conclusion for the mighty fugue, commonly regarded as the culmination of polyphonic composition.
2. A choral piece, *L'Aurore*, which also contained forbidden parallelisms, in this case, a long chain of parallel octaves in the outer voice parts.

The judges were not amused. One of them, Émile Paladilhe, remarked that they would not tolerate being taken as imbeciles.

Did Ravel not realize, as Debussy did while at the Conservatoire, that you had to follow the rules in order to get ahead? Or, having reached the age of thirty in 1905, was Ravel now openly defying the Conservatoire, which was known for keeping its distance from contemporary musical styles? According to his friends and supporters, there was yet another reason for the judges' decision: they were showing their condemnation of Ravel's earlier compositions that had brought him both initial acclaim and controversy. These works included *Sites auriculaires* (1895–1897), *Shéhérazade* (1898), *Jeux d'eau* (1901), and the String Quartet (1902–1903); all four compositions had been performed at concerts of the Société Nationale de musique. Another important early work, his first popular success, was the *Pavane pour une infante défunte* (*Pavane for a Dead Princess*). Written in 1899, this solo piece for piano was introduced to the public by his good friend Ricardo Viñes at the Salle Pleyel in 1902. Ravel's orchestral version appeared later in 1910.

Regarding the premiere of *Shéhérazade*, for example, Ravel reported in a letter dated June 9, 1899, to his friend Florent Schmitt, "*Shéhérazade* was strongly booed. They applauded also, and in all honesty I must admit that the applauders were more numerous than the protestors, because I was called back twice. Moreover, d'Indy, whose behavior toward me was first-rate, was delighted that people could still become impassioned about anything." Whatever the exact reason or reasons may have been, the judges' decision to pass over Ravel at the preliminary level of the 1905 contest helped to ignite a scandal that became known as the first *Affaire Ravel*.

THE FIRST *L'AFFAIRE RAVEL*

The scandal arose from two decisions made by the five-member jury in May 1905: (1) they rejected Ravel and another previous finalist, Hélène Fleury, who were pupils of Gabriel Fauré and Charles-Marie Widor, respectively; and (2) all six finalists they selected were students of Charles Lenepveu, a member of the jury who was well known for his arch-conservatism in music and hostility to innovation.

The jury's decision reached scandal status when the music critics of important publications, such as *Le Matin* and *Le Mercure musical*, shouted foul, as did Ravel himself. In a long interview published in the May 22, 1905, issue of *Le Matin*, he stated that Lenepveu should have recused himself from the jury. He pointed out that of the nineteen candidates presented to the jury that year, eight of them were students of Lenepveu, and six of these advanced to the final round. In other words, students of other Conservatoire teachers were not selected. As it was true then, so it is true today: the judges' decisions appeared arbitrary and smacked of unfairness.

The judges never reversed their decision, but the sequel to the scandal was a major reorganization at the Conservatoire. Although the director, Théodore Dubois, had announced his intention to resign from his post a couple of months earlier, the choice of his replacement that June was surprising. It was Ravel's teacher, Gabriel Fauré, who was something of an outsider. A gifted composer, he had not attended the Conservatoire but the Ecole Niedermeyer, which specialized in religious music. Nor had he ever won the Prix de Rome. At one point in his career, he was considered for the position of professor of composition at the Conservatoire. Ultimately, he was not selected because his music was deemed by then-Conservatoire head Ambroise Thomas as too modern.

When Fauré was appointed head of the Conservatoire in 1905, a position he was to hold for the next fifteen years, he began a number of sweeping reforms that strengthened and broadened the Conservatoire's curricula. Singers were henceforth required to develop proficiency in rhythm and take courses in diction and sight-reading. Instrumentalists had to learn solfège. Music history was now a required course for all students.

Fauré also reformed the administrative side of the Conservatoire. External judges were secured for competitions, no doubt to avoid future charges of favoritism. The governing council of the institution was also expanded. Even Debussy, the former rebel of the Conservatoire who then as now personifies the independent-minded musician, was invited to join the governing council in 1909—evidence that under Fauré the institution was indeed broadening its vision. No one was more surprised by this offer than Debussy. In an interview which appeared in the February 14, 1909, issue of *Le Figaro*, he stated, "'The most surprised person at this nomination for membership of the Conseil Supérieur of the Conservatoire is, I assure you, your own obedient servant,' he said to me at once. 'I have never before been called to sit on such a jury, never before have the higher spheres of officialdom solicited my collaboration. So I am literally dumbfounded'" (*DOM*, 236). Debussy may have been shocked to find himself on an upper level of the music establishment, but it is clear that he was in some agreement with Fauré's curriculum changes. For one, Debussy thought that the vocal instruction could stand improvement.

> Ah! those [instrumental classes] are perfect. No other instrumentalists in the world equal the French.
>
> I do not, however, have the same admiration for the singing classes. Our singers are generally badly taught. The students go to the singing classes but they never go, or rarely go, to the *sol-fa* classes.

As for Ravel, the scandal did not adversely affect his reputation, career, or productivity. On the contrary, it created more interest and boosted both his confidence and career. Just a few weeks after the scandal broke in the news in May 1905, a wealthy businessman named Alfred Edwards and his wife Misia took Ravel on a seven-week canal trip though France, Belgium, Holland, and Germany on board his 120-foot yacht.

Subsequently, that September, the publishing house of Durand et Cie offered Ravel an exclusive contract; henceforth, almost all of his works would be published by Durand. More than that, Ravel now entered what was perhaps the productive period in life. In the decade following the scandal, he produced some of his most famous works. These works include *Miroirs* for piano (1905), *L'Heure espagnole*, a one-act opera based on a libretto by Franc-Nohain (1907–1909), *Rapsodie espagnole* for orchestra (1907–1908), *Gaspard de la nuit* for piano (1908), *Ma mere l'Oye* (*Mother Goose*) for piano four hands (1908–1910), and the ballet *Daphnis et Chloé* (1909–1912).

In the final twist of irony, once Fauré assumed leadership of the Conservatoire, he arranged for Ravel to serve on various juries, including the one for the Prix de Rome. Today, Ravel's music is frequently included in the audition repertoire for conservatories and music schools around the world.

DEBUSSY AND RAVEL

As mentioned above, the relationship between Debussy and Ravel was complex and shifted through several different phases. The lack of any correspondence between them adds a layer of mystery to their biographies but also suggests that they never became close friends. We do know that they moved in the same circles and had common friends, including the composer Erik Satie and the pianist Ricardo Viñes.

Les Apaches

Initially, Ravel looked up to the older Debussy and was one of his most ardent supporters. They, along with Viñes, were members of a group of French musicians, poets, artists, and critics dubbed Les Apaches, which began in 1902–1903 and met weekly. The unusual name was coined by Viñes to describe his group of "artistic outcasts." He had adapted the name from a gang of Parisian hoodlums, described in the newspapers of the time as violent and known for using head-butt and hooding tactics for robbing people. The name was also a reference to the tribe of Native American Indians who were regarded as fierce and aggressive warriors.

What drew this artistic group of Apaches together were interests in Chinese art, Russian music, French folk songs, Symbolist poems and texts, and the promotion of new and innovative French compositions. Of special importance was the music of Claude Debussy. He was their idol, which explains why they spent a good deal of time and effort helping to get *Pelléas et Mélisande* off the ground in 1902. Their tactics that year were threefold. First, the group tried to attend every performance of the initial run of Debussy's opera at the Opéra-Comique. In so doing, they established a solid block of support from the outset. Second, from the cheapest seats of the house (five francs per ticket), they enthusiastically clapped when the rest of the audience appeared to be lukewarm. Third, they each brought along a friend to generate further interest in the opera. Thanks in part to the Apaches' three-prong strategy of support, enthusiasm, and recruitment, Debussy's controversial opera was able to launch. In the *Histoire de la musique* (1949), Emile Vuillermoz had this to say about Debussy's "sacred battalion":

Their devotion was not useless . . . for the incomprehension and irony of the majority of the public would have rendered the exploitation of the work impossible if this "sacred battalion" had not come to each and every performance during long months to insure there were police in the hall and to keep an atmosphere of infectious enthusiasm up until the moment when the opera could, without danger, pursue its career alone.

Stylistic Connections

What binds Debussy and Ravel together and distinguishes them from other French composers of the time is a whole network of connections. A few of these have already been mentioned or alluded to earlier in this chapter, to wit, their rigorous training at the Paris Conservatoire, initially as piano majors; their friendship with Satie and Viñes; their membership in Les Apaches and the Société Nationale; and a shared interest in Edgar Allan Poe and the Symbolist writers. Russian, Spanish, and Asian music also affected their musical language. Some of their many other commonalities are as follows.

They wrote in many of the same genres, sometimes producing the same number of compositions per genre. That is, Debussy and Ravel each composed one string quartet, with the second movement a pizzicato scherzo. Each man wrote a single piano trio, and each set three poems by Mallarmé in the same year (1913). In 1909, Debussy published *Children's Corner*, a six-movement suite for piano. Similarly, just one year later, Ravel came out with his *Mother Goose*, a five-movement suite for piano duet.

They both excelled at orchestration, and they enjoyed combining and adjusting sounds in novel ways. Sometimes they would cast instruments typically used in a secondary capacity in a solo position. Two examples: the harp solos in Debussy's *Danse sacrée et danse profane* (1904) and Ravel's *Introduction et Allegro* (1905). Concomitantly, they would reduce the sound volume of other instruments, whether by muting the strings and brass or by eliminating doublings (i.e., instruments duplicating the music played by other instruments). They also took fresh approaches to traditional instruments, such as by exploiting the extreme registers of the piano keyboard or by asking wind players to execute harmonics (partial pitches).

Their expertise and flair for orchestration helped to draw public attention to the music of less experienced orchestrators. Debussy orchestrated two of Satie's three *Gymnopédies* in 1897, while Ravel orchestrated Mussorgsky's *Pictures at an Exhibition* in 1922. Arguably, these orchestrated versions are better known than the original versions for solo piano. Ravel, more so than Debussy, tended to focus on the virtuosic capabilities of individual instruments.

They both eschewed the heavy chromaticism that dominated so many scores of contemporary German composers as well as the French Wagnerians. Instead, Debussy and Ravel tended to employ a variety of nontraditional sonorities, such as quartal, quintal, and extended tertian chords (ninths, elevenths, thirteenths, etc.). While it is true that extended tertian chords appeared in the works of earlier composers, such as Chopin and Liszt, these sounds can be heard more extensively in Debussy and Ravel's music. Ravel also venture more often into the area of polytonality, pushing the boundaries of tonal music even further. Polytonality results when two or more keys sound at the same time so that the music divides into different layers of tonality.

They both avoided the strict use of traditional seven-note, major and minor scales. They preferred more unusual formations, such as the pentatonic, octatonic, and whole-tone scales. Similarly, both men helped to resurrect the ancient Greek modes, the distant ancestors of the Western scales, by reintroducing them into their respective compositions. In his *Menuet antique* (1895), for instance, Ravel used the Dorian mode, as did Debussy in his *Prelude to "The Afternoon of a Faun."*

Ravel and Debussy's revival of the past was not just limited to modes. To be sure, both men often and consciously drew upon many other stylistic attributes of earlier times. Ravel, in particular, wrote mostly homophonic textures, regular and steady rhythms, clear melodies, simpler forms, and obvious cadences. In so doing, he was reacting to the rhetoric of late Romantic music, with its thick textures, unending melodies, and general impression of excess. Both men favored the aesthetics and techniques of classical and earlier periods of music. Their preference for clarity, order, and restraint would prevail in Stravinsky's neoclassical works of the 1920s and beyond.

Yet another commonality was their penchant for harmonic parallelism, also known as planing or parallel voice leading. In earlier periods of tonal music, certain kinds of movement between adjacent vertical intervals or chords were forbidden, especially parallel fifths and root position triads. The reason behind this rule had to do with flow. If the top note of a perfect fifth interval, for example, moves up while the lower note moves down (or vice versa), what results is contrary motion. This is the preferred way because the two notes sound as if they are moving independently. Whereas if both top and bottom notes of the perfect fifth move up together (or, vice versa, down together) to another perfect fifth, the result is parallel motion. The two sets of parallel fifths sound as if they are stuck together.

Both Debussy and Ravel were among the first composers to exploit harmonic parallelism in the late nineteenth- and twentieth-century classical music. True, there are examples of earlier instances of this construction in tonal music, such as Chopin's *Mazurka*, op. 24, no. 2 (1835), but Debussy and Ravel were the first composers of the time to use it extensively throughout their respective outputs. The degree of harmonic parallelism could vary from piece to piece. Sometimes they would just write a set of parallel chords or a measure full of them. Other times, they would write long chains of parallel chords. The effect produced must have been strange or refreshing back then, depending on the inclination of the listener.

As to why Debussy and Ravel employed harmonic parallelism so extensively in their music, it is not clear. Their decision may be connected to the rise of neoclassicism in late nineteenth-century music in Europe. In the case of harmonic parallelism, the inspiration might have been the parallel harmonies (i.e., organum) of medieval music.

Toward Understanding the Differences between Debussy and Ravel

Back in the early 1990s, I had just completed my dissertation on Debussy's sonata forms and was employed by the Chicago Symphony Orchestra (CSO) Association as a member of the development department. One of the perks of my office job was the opportunity to attend free performances of classical music by the CSO, which consisted of some of the best musicians in the world. On one occasion, I heard Ravel's *Boléro* in Orchestra Hall. I remember that the audience was smiling and eagerly waiting in hushed excitement for the piece to begin, as if under a spell. First, we heard a distinctive Spanish rhythm, played *pianissimo* by a single snare drum while the violas and cellos played a simple pizzicato accompaniment. Next, we heard two different melodies. The first, played by a solo flute, was long, mostly stepwise, and in the key of C major; it was immediately repeated by another wind instrument, the clarinet. The second melody, played as a bassoon solo, was just as long, yet it seemed more intense and exotic to me, in part because it was syncopated, with emphasis placed on a "strange" pitch. (Later I learned the exotic sound could also be attributed to the Phrygian mode of this melody, a mode often used in much Spanish and Arabic music. The strange pitch that I heard reiterated was the flatted second step, i.e., D ♭ or Phrygian second, of the C mode.)

Over the course of this one-movement piece, I noticed that these two melodies were constantly repeated, one after the other, each time with different instrumentation. It was as if every member of the orchestra was getting a chance to shine, including some rather unusual instruments for the time: the oboe d'amore, sopranino saxophone, piccolo trumpet, and tenor saxophone. Eventually, I realized that a huge instrumental pile-up was gradually and steadily taking shape through a series of variations. By the end of the one-movement piece, all the instruments had combined to produce an enormous and awe-inspiring sound. Yet, not for a moment during the entire seventeen-minute length of the work did the distinctive Spanish rhythm from the opening measures ever disappear. Like the two melodies, it was constantly repeated, delivering a hypnotic effect.

What I remember about watching the live performance of *Boléro* was how bored some musicians on the stage appeared to be, especially the members of the first violin section. I can now understand why: historically, the string section was the backbone of the orchestra and the violins, in particular, were often assigned the melody of the primary theme. In contrast, during at least the entire first half of *Boléro*, the first violins were silent. Moreover, when they finally made their entrance, they were in the background providing harmonic accompaniment and playing divisi and pizzicato notes, as if they are tiptoeing into the piece. It was well into the second half of *Boléro* before the first violin section was assigned the melody. For me, this was an exciting moment to experience: to see the usual leaders of the orchestra show everyone just how well they could play the melody, so clearly and strongly.

Another takeaway from that first performance was the unusual overall design of the piece. I noticed that Ravel had constructed a single,
enormous crescendo, with interest generated by the various orchestral
colors and combinations. But once the entire orchestra was playing
altogether and the sound level was loud, I wondered where the piece
would go from here. Become even louder? Collapse into silence?

Ravel was clever. He skirted the obvious solutions and went in another direction—literally. In the penultimate variation of the piece, he
abruptly broke free from C major, the one and only key thus far, and
modulated upward to a "new" key of E major. (In point of fact, E major
was foreshadowed in a previous variation; however, it was somewhat
hidden in a polytonal setting, whereby three keys [C, G, and E majors]
sound simultaneously rather than one at a time. It would take careful
listening to separate and identify the different key layers.) The modula-
tion was not only abrupt; it was also brief because for the last variation
of the piece, Ravel returned to the home key of C major with a wild and
giant fanfare. This brief, sideways digression, I thought, was both clever
and effective since it gave additional energy to the expanding trajectory
of the piece.

I have shared memories of my first hearing of Ravel's *Boléro* as a
way of illustrating a few of the essential differences between Debussy
and Ravel. For a start, Ravel's melodies are generally longer and his
forms more clearly articulated and hard-edged; it is relatively easy for
listeners to determine the beginnings and endings of his phrases and
sections. In addition, his music features a great deal of literal repetition,
to such an extent that it can tend to sound mechanical. With regard to
Boléro, he identified a specific factory that was his source of inspiration.
It was located in Le Vésinet, a suburb outside Paris.

By contrast, Debussy's melodies were usually quite brief and fleeting, his forms less clearly defined. He tended to keep all literal repetition to a minimum. He would never have written an obvious yet clever
piece like *Boléro* that is, in essence, a steady crescendo with an unexpected twist. He preferred to write works of wondrous and mysterious
beauty. As evidence, consider the following passage from one of his last
articles, entitled "Taste," which he wrote for the bulletin of the Société
internationale de musique (*SIM*) in 1913: "We should constantly be
reminding ourselves that the beauty of a work of art is something that
will always remain mysterious; that is to say one can never find out

exactly 'how it is done.' At all costs let us preserve this element of magic peculiar to music. By its very nature music is more likely to contain something of the magical than any other art."

The concept of offsetting a lucid design with the element of surprise was not unique to *Boléro*. Rather, it was one of Ravel's guiding aesthetic principles. (The fact that he decorated the yellow walls of his bedroom with graceful but upside-down Ionic columns suggests that his musical aesthetics extended into the interior design of his private home.) Although *Boléro* was composed in 1928, a decade after Debussy's death, it is entirely possible that he would not have been impressed. This is because Debussy disliked Ravel's way of creating magic tricks, of pulling the rug out from listeners' expectations.

At first, Debussy was intrigued with Ravel's music. Regarding the score of Ravel's *Histoires naturelles*, Debussy wrote the following remarks in a February 25, 1907, letter to his editor Jacques Durand: "Thank you for the *Histoires naturelles* . . . it's an extremely curious score! It's artificial and chimerical, rather like the house of a wizard!" (*Letters*, 177).

Then he became annoyed. Just a few weeks later, in a March 8, 1907, letter to his friend Louis Laloy, Debussy wrote,

> I agree with you Ravel is extraordinarily gifted, but what annoys me is the attitude he adopts of being a "conjuror" [faiseur de tours], or rather a Fakir casting spells and making flowers burst out of chairs. . . . The trouble is, a conjuring trick always has to have a build-up and after you've seen it once you're no longer astonished.
>
> For the moment I'm happy if people find it entertaining. Given the way people torment and annoy music, she might be glad to hear the excuse that her only function is to bring a smile to the lips!

Boléro became immensely popular. Success was fueled in part because of the 1934 film *Bolero*, which featured actors Carole Lombard and George Raft dancing seductively to an abbreviated version of Ravel's *Boléro*. Decades later, the music was featured again in the 1980 film *10*, during the scene where Jenny (Bo Derek) makes love to George (Dudley Moore). Both films were box office hits. Ravel, however, conceived *Boléro* as a ballet score for the Russian dancer and actress Ida Rubenstein. He wanted the ballet to take place in front of a factory, with workers dancing together. Rubenstein had a different conception in mind: for the premiere performance at the Paris Opéra in 1928, she portrayed a female gypsy dancing on a table surrounded by men in a Spanish bar.

THE SECOND *L'AFFAIRE RAVEL*

In 1904 a rift began to form between Debussy and Ravel, one that had to do with arguments over music plagiarism and priority. That year, Ravel claimed that Debussy stole the principal idea from Ravel's "Habanera" and then used it in the composition "La soirée dans Grenade." Ravel made another accusation in 1906, this time complaining that he—and not Debussy—was the first to write more innovative piano music, citing his *Jeux d'eau* as the seminal work. The second *Affaire Ravel* erupted the following year in the French press—a war of words that intensified an ongoing controversy about the stylistic and technical similarities between Debussy and Ravel.

The following is a timeline of the first of two pivotal aspects leading up to the height of the second *Affaire Ravel*, which was in 1907. The first aspect is sometimes known as the Habanera Incident, and the four compositions that played a role in particular were Ravel's *Sites auriculaires* and *Rapsodie espagnole*, and Debussy's *Lindaraja* and *Estampes*.

The Habanera Incident

1895–1897   Ravel composes *Sites auriculaires* for two pianos. The title literally means "places sensed by the ear." The two pieces in the set are "Habanera" and "Entre cloches." On the autograph manuscript of "Habanera" is the date 1895. *Sites auriculaires* constitutes the first public performance of a work by Ravel, but the work will remain unpublished until 1975.

1898   *Sites auriculaires* is performed on March 5 by Ricardo Viñes and Marthe Dron at a Société nationale concert in the Salle Pleyel. Claude Debussy is reportedly in attendance. After the concert, Debussy asks Ravel for permission to borrow the score of the first movement,

"Habanera." Given Debussy's long-standing appreciation of Spanish music, his request is understandable. Ravel loans him the score, which Debussy does not return until years later.

1901 In April, Debussy composes *Lindaraja*, a one-movement piece for two pianos that was neither performed nor published during his lifetime. The composer himself may have withheld the composition from publication, possibly because a substantial portion of the piece (i.e., 24 of 185 measures) "resembles" the "Habanera" of Ravel's *Sites auriculaires*.

1903 Between July and October, Debussy completes the *Estampes* (*Engravings*), a three-movement work for piano. The second movement, "La soirée dans Granade" ("Evening in Grenada"), also has the same combination of connections to Ravel's "Habanera."

1904 The premiere of Debussy's "La soirée dans Grenade" at the Société nationale takes place on January 9. Ravel complains to his friend Madame de Saint-Marceaux that Debussy stole from him the principal idea of "Habanera," a piece he had composed ten years ago.

Monsieur Lalo and *Jeux d'eau*

The second pivotal aspect leading to the height of the second *Affaire Ravel* was Pierre Lalo's negative coverage of Ravel's music, especially in the years following the first *Affaire Ravel*. Lalo (1866–1943) was a Parisian music critic who wrote for the daily *Le Temps*. He is remembered most for his sharp, witty, and sometimes offensive reviews. He was one of Debussy's first supporters, though his reviews of the composer's later music, such as *La mer*, were less positive, if not cutting.

With regard to Ravel, Lalo was plainly hostile. He consistently accused Ravel of imitating Debussy and other composers. In his January 30, 1906, review, for instance, Lalo wrote about Ravel's "very apparent and rather annoying faults" and "the strange resemblance of his music to that of M. Claude Debussy," a resemblance that was both "extreme" and "striking." Ravel became upset. Like most young artists, he was anxious to assert his own voice and musical authority; he did not want to be viewed as derivative.

The cut that hurt Ravel the most was Lalo's opinion that Debussy had "created a new manner of writing for the keyboard, a special style of particular virtuosity." Ravel responded privately to Lalo in a letter dated February 5, 1906, and quoted in Arbie Orenstein's *A Ravel Reader: Correspondence, Articles, Interviews*. In this letter, Ravel contended that he was indeed a true original. As evidence, he pointed out that his *Jeux d'eau* of 1902 was more innovative than anything that Debussy had written thus far for piano. Ravel explained that while he had a "deep admiration" for Debussy's piano compositions, "from a purely pianistic point of view, they contain nothing new."

Ravel's letter did not sway Lalo. In point of fact, the following year the friction between the two men intensified. In the March 19, 1907, issue of *Le Temps*, Lalo gave a negative review of Ravel's *Histoires naturelles*, a song cycle about animals, finding it "laborious and precious and dry, and also almost as lacking in real music—a collection of industrious rarities and a succession of reversed and complicated chords." Later in the same article, Lalo excoriated the latest generation of young composers (by implication, Ravel), claiming they committed plagiarism and essentially describing them as cardboard musicians. Lalo also stated that these young composers regarded Debussy as old school and aimed to marginalize him:

> What is there in common between [Debussy's] art, which flowed from the very source of poetic sentiment, and the art of the diligent little composers who claim this art as their own? They do not feel nature in the least: in none of their works have they succeeded in evoking nature. They have no human feeling. They have never expressed an emotion or passion of a human soul. They do nothing but write notes, combinations of chords, and the tone coloring of different instruments; they have in common with Debussy only the technique of composing. And this technique they have borrowed directly from him. . . .
>
> These young people, by the way, do more than just claim a part in M. Debussy's art. They have recently begun to push M. Debussy out of "Debussysm," they have begun to isolate him, even to discard him altogether, to point out to him that his part in it is finished, that he has, hereafter, nothing to do with this business, since he never did

have much to do with it of any importance. "The house belongs to us and it is up to you to leave."

Ravel was furious. A few weeks later, he sent a letter of complaint to the editor of *Le Temps*, which was published in the April 9, 1907, issue. In his letter Ravel not only issued a formal denial to Lalo but also—perhaps unwisely—challenged him to produce a witness who heard him make any disparaging remarks about Debussy.

Ravel's reaction to Lalo's review is understandable. After all, he was defending his art and reputation. In hindsight, however, he should have ignored Lalo's negative assessment of his music because the savvy critic's next attack was even more harsh and aggressive. It was one of the missives that helped to bring the war of words in France to a whole new level.

At the Height of the Controversy

Lalo's "witness" was none other than Ravel himself. Apparently, Lalo had saved Ravel's February 5, 1906, letter for over a year, biding his time before revealing the contents to the public in the April 9, 1907, issue of *Le Temps*, right beside Ravel's latest letter. He used Ravel's own words against him. A full paragraph of Ravel's earlier letter to Lalo, which could be read as disparaging toward Debussy, will now be reproduced here:

> I would like to call your impartial attention to the following point. You expatiate at some length upon a certain type of writing for the piano, whose invention you ascribe to Debussy. But the *Jeux d'eau* appeared at the beginning of 1902, at a time when there were only "Three pieces for piano" composed by Debussy, for which, I do not need to tell you, I have a passionate admiration, but works which from a purely pianistic point of view did not bring anything new. I hope you will excuse this legitimate claim.

Thereafter, the Debussy-Ravel imbroglio was a point of contention in the press, with some of the era's leading critics forming opposing camps. Léon Vallas was an ardent supporter of Debussy, while Gaston Carraud was an equally ardent supporter of Ravel. Most critics, however, were not as extremely polarized. While they argued over whether

Ravel had imitated Debussy or not, they also articulated the two composers' differences in compositional styles. Louis Laloy was one of those French music critics who had a more nuanced understanding of Debussy and Ravel's music. In an insightful article that appeared in the June 1, 1904, issue of *La Revue musicale*, Laloy wrote that Ravel's "music is not an imitative music; it has a personal accent and, in particular, shows evidence of a taste for pictorial detail which is not encountered in Monsieur Debussy." Laloy was also one of the first listeners to note that Ravel's harmonies were even more daring than Debussy: "No one has pushed the art of substitutions, alterations and unexpected convergences as far as [Ravel]—to the farthest limit where the chord, at the point of breaking apart, still remains in balance, and always obeys the rational principle of tonality: everything is surprising and everything can be explained."

At the Heart of the Matter

As we approach the end of this chapter, there is at least one question that remains to be answered: was there any truth to Ravel's claim that Debussy stole the principal idea from his "Habanera"? The best way to answer this question is by listening to Ravel's "Habanera" and then comparing it to Debussy's "La soirée dans Grenade."

Listen closely to just the opening measures of the Ravel, for approximately thirty seconds; this seven-measure introduction will be the major point of contention. Notice especially these two features: (1) a relentless habanera rhythm (triplet, duplet) on a C♯ harp pedal point clashing with (2) arpeggiated augmented sixth chords on G and D.

Now listen to the first minute or so of Debussy's "La soirée dans Grenade." (The 1969 RAI recording featuring pianist Martha Argerich is one option.) Do not expect to hear the connection between the Debussy and Ravel pieces right away because the material Debussy supposedly lifted is somewhat buried. That is, the "lifted material" is the fourth of five main elements in the first two sections of the Debussy, the introduction followed by an A section. The five main elements, in order of presentation, are as follows:

0:00   A six-measure introduction that presents a simpler variant of the habanera rhythm (TUM-Ta-TUM-TUM). Like

Ravel, Debussy reiterates the distinctive rhythm on the same note, C♯, functioning as the dominant of the tonic key of F♯ minor.

0:15   The start of the A section, which begins with an "exotic" melody that brings to mind flamenco music

0:35   Parallel seventh chords that are based on another exotic scale, the whole tone, and rise in a lower, darker range

0:45   A different series of rising whole-tone chords rising in a higher range. The first chord of the series is an incomplete dominant seventh chord on G, the enharmonic equivalent of an augmented sixth chord, clashing with habanera rhythm on the C♯ pedal point. It is this combination of unusual features—the augmented chord on G in a tritone dissonance with the reiterated C♯ habanera rhythm—that is the most incriminating piece of evidence against Debussy. A repeat of the parallel seventh chords follows at 0:57.

1:05   A descending series of parallel chords

The short answer is, yes, Ravel's "Habanera" is the source from which Debussy reused six measures for his "La soirée dans Grenade." The similarities are too unique or unusual to be a coincidence. Still, the two pieces are very different in terms of technique and development. This is the conclusion I reached after listening to both of them in their entirety. For one thing, in the Ravel, the habanera rhythm is relentless; with the exception of two measures, it can be heard in every measure of his piece. By contrast, in the Debussy, the habanera rhythm disappears from time to time, such as when the mysterious parallel seventh chords emerge briefly only to disappear in the ebb and flow of the night, or when, toward the end of the piece, a series of mostly major parallel triads playfully flashes forth, though it too disappears, as quickly as it arose. To me, this crosscutting technique helped Debussy to capture the nightlife on an island in the Caribbean. I can see myself sitting at an outdoor café, listening for the most part to the soft music of a Spanish guitar. From time to time, my attention is diverted elsewhere—by shadowy figures in the far corner of the café or by a child running past me. But for the most part, I am focused on the music and enjoy being slowly lulled into a relaxed state of mind.

Another important difference is that the Debussy seems to be more complex. In terms of design, for instance, "La soirée dans Grenade" follows a five-part A–B–C–B'–A'. It also features several smaller-scale units that thread their way through the course of the piece. In the Ravel, by comparison, there are just two sections, A–A', the second a variation of the first. There are bold and imaginative points, such as the Andalusian-style progression from F♯ minor to F♯ major at the ends of the two sections. However, these points do not interrupt the hypnotic effect of the piece; rather, they are layered onto the score. Debussy prefers to develop ideas, cutting back and forth among them to make changes as well as connections; in this, he may have been inspired by the crosscutting techniques common to the silent movies of his time. His rather snide comment about another piece by Ravel, the *Valses nobles et sentimentales*, confirms the view that development was central to Debussy's composition approach: "A good deal more can be done with that music!"

DEBUSSY AND RAVEL IN PERSPECTIVE

Clearly, Ravel was upset not just about the accusations of plagiarism leveled against him but also because his own innovations were not being taken that seriously. Why else, then, would he add the date 1895 to the 1908 score of the orchestral version of "Habanera"? (That year, "Habanera" was published as part of *Rapsodie espagnole*, and it was the only movement of the work marked with a date.) This can only be construed as a defiant gesture made by Ravel to substantiate his precedence as an innovator and his legitimacy as a composer. He was also trying to get back at his critics.

As for Debussy, he seemed not to have been overly preoccupied with the controversy. Ravel's name appeared only twice in Debussy's letters dating from 1907, in the discussions with Jacques Durand and Louis Laloy cited above. In both letters, Debussy referred to Ravel as a kind of magician. In all likelihood, Debussy's attention was focused elsewhere. He was now the doting father of a young daughter, Claude-Emma "Chouchou" Debussy, born October 30, 1905. We do know that Debussy and Ravel eventually stopped visiting each other, and mutual friends such as Louis Laloy vouched for the fact that both composers regretted the rupture.

Yet the controversy must have bothered Debussy. While he never referred to it directly, in either published form or private correspondence, the remarks he made in a 1913 article for *SIM* could be read as a belated response to the accusation of plagiarism made by Ravel and his supporters a few years earlier:

> One architect would never dream of reproaching another for having used the same kind of stone as himself. Nonetheless, would he not be shocked to find formal similarities in the work of a colleague? It is evidently not the case in music, where a modern composer can copy the forms of some classical work without anything turning a hair. He's even to be congratulated for it! (Respect for tradition manifests itself in some very strange ways.) But as soon as he uses a so-called forbidden chord, the public cries, "Stop, thief!" To put it another way: one chord, even if it's from a monumental piece of music, has no more importance in itself than one stone in a fine building. It's where it is placed that counts, and the way it throws into relief the flowing curves of the melodic line.

Several conclusions can be drawn from the above statements. Above all, it seems that Debussy did not believe that copying a small amount of material from another composer was an example of plagiarism. Since architects do this all the time, he reasoned, composers should also feel free to copy another composer's material, as long as they treat or develop it in a new and different way.

Debussy's rationale makes perfect sense to us. In the current age of mixes, mash-ups, and remixes, the repurposing of a musical idea might seem to be a nonissue. For us, musical creativity does not necessarily mean inventing an idea out of thin air; what a musician does with borrowed material is just as acceptable. It is possible that Debussy was pulling away from the Romantic notion of originality, which held that truly original work was to be created from nothingness, and was thinking in more modern terms.

FINAL THOUGHTS

Despite the rupture in their friendship due to the second *L'affaire Ravel*, Debussy and Ravel maintained a lifelong respect for each other. Debussy thought Ravel was "extraordinarily gifted," while Ravel held Debussy in great esteem. In 1918, Ravel attended Debussy's funeral procession, a symbol of respect. In his 1928 lecture on contemporary music at Rice University in Texas, Ravel stated that Debussy was "the most phenomenal genius in the history of French music." In a 1931 interview, Ravel gave what is perhaps his most moving compliment about Debussy's music: his dearest wish would be "to die gently lulled in the tender and voluptuous embrace of Claude Debussy's *Prelude to The Afternoon of a Faun.*"

5

THE WATER MUSIC

Debussy had a lifelong fascination with water, especially the sea. Free flowing, beautiful, ever changing, nuanced, mysterious—the sea was the ideal showcase for his unique talents. His musical landscapes (or waterscapes) include some of his most famous works: the song *Le jet d'eau* (*The Water Jet*, 1889), "En bateau" (*Sailing*, 1889), "Le tombeau des naïades" ("The Tomb of the Water Nymphs," 1899), "Sirènes" (1901), *La mer* (*The Sea*, 1905), "Reflets dans l'eau" ("Reflections in the Water," 1905), *L'isle joyeuse* (*The Island of Joy*, 1904), "Voiles" ("Veils" or "Sails," 1909), "La cathédrale engloutie" ("The Submerged Cathedral," 1910), and "Ondine" (1913). Other Debussy works, such as "Poissons d'or" ("Goldfish," 1907), imply or express the element of water.

In many ways, his personal life also connected with water. Displayed on a wall in Debussy's office was a print of Katsushika Hokusai's famous woodblock *The Great Wave off Kanogawa*. A portion of Hokusai's *Great Wave* was also reproduced on the cover of the first edition of *La mer*. He also sought refuge by the sea during one of the worst crises of his life, the dissolution of his first marriage. This was in early August 1904, when Debussy left his wife of more than four years, a pretty model and dressmaker named Lilly Texier, for a married woman with two children. Her name was Emma Bardac. She and Debussy ran away to the island of Jersey, off the coast of Normandy, where they stayed incognito at the Grand Hotel on the main esplanade. After traveling to other coastal towns in Normandy, the couple returned to Paris in mid-October. Shortly thereafter, Lilly Debussy attempted suicide by shoot-

ing herself in the stomach. The following year Debussy and Emma
Bardac obtained divorces from the respective spouses. They did not
marry until January 1908, more than two years after the birth of their
daughter Claude-Emma Debussy, who was called Chouchou ("dar-
ling").

Debussy and Emma would return to Normandy in the summer of
1911, this time with Chouchou. They spent their family holiday at
Houlgate. One could go so far as to say that Debussy had a lifetime
engagement with the sea. As he wrote in his letter to André Messager
on September 12, 1903, "You're unaware, maybe, that I was intended
for the noble career of a sailor and have only deviated from that path
thanks to the quirks of fate. Even so, I've retained a sincere devotion to
the sea" (*Letters*, 141).

Among the many composers of water music, Debussy stands apart.
We now turn to three works that will demonstrate his extraordinary
ability to convey the mysterious attraction of the sea.

VOILES

Debussy wrote twenty-four preludes for solo piano, divided into two
books of twelve preludes each. Book 1 appeared in 1910, and book 2 in
1913. As such, they represent some of his last works for piano. Unlike
some other collections of preludes, notably those by Johann Sebastian
Bach, Chopin, and Shostakovich, Debussy's are not cyclical; they do not
adhere to a systematic succession of keys, nor are Debussy's preludes
paired with fugues. One commonality is that the printed titles appear at
the ends of each prelude, as if they were indications of origins or,
conversely, afterthoughts. *Voiles*, the title of the second prelude of book
1, is also ambiguous. This French word has two possible meanings,
translating into English as either "sails" or "veils." Thus, Debussy may
have been inspired by sailboats or the swirling veils of dancers. He
never explained, nor would we have expected him to, since ambiguity
was basic to his aesthetic. Whenever I listen to this piece, I opt for the
first meaning; I imagine a boat sailing slowly in the fog. Try listening to
Voiles without the score and open your mind to these possible interpretations of the music.

There are several plausible reasons for hearing *Voiles* as a musical depiction of, or an allusion to, a seascape. First of all, the outer A sections of the piece are limited to the whole-tone scale, which consists of six whole steps: C–D–E–F♯–G♯–A♯ (and their enharmonic equivalents). Because these tones are equidistant from each other, no one tone stands out in terms of importance. The effect is one of weightlessness or floating. Significantly, Debussy did not include a key signature, at least at the outset of the piece, as if to avoid setting a key. Now, it is possible that B♭ is the key center of *Voiles* because this pitch sounds throughout the work in a low register; it is a point of emphasis, perhaps alluding to the floor of the sea. Even during the contrasting middle B section, when the key signatures moves to five flats (B♭ minor? D♭ major?) and when Debussy presents the minor pentatonic mode on E♭, the B♭ pedal still sounds below. Interestingly, during the last three measures of the piece, the B♭ pedal disappears, and the concluding notes are C and E. It is tempting to imagine that at the end of *Voiles* the sailboat is finally and completely adrift.

The uncertainty created by the whole-tone scale in the outer A sections is mirrored by metric ambiguity. The notated meter may be 2/4, but what we hear is a variety of metrical groupings. In the first few measures alone, the meter for the right-hand part can be heard as duple, while the B♭ pedal points sound in groups of three and four. It is only in the central B section that we hear regular metrical groupings of the B♭ pedal in the left-hand part. *Note:* we have already seen this large-scale trajectory whereby the music moves from structural irregularity or ambiguity in the opening section to solidification and clarity in the central section, in works such as the *Prelude to "The Afternoon of a Faun."* This fluid "process of becoming" is another hallmark of Debussy's style of composition and one that can be traced back to earlier composers, such as Schumann, Schubert, and Beethoven.

The ambiguous and floating sound is just a single aspect of *Voiles*. Also intrinsic to the work are the oscillation patterns that replicate wavelike currents. Listen to the piece again, this time focusing on the ascending and descending directions of the melodic ideas in the opening measures. Notice that the upper melody at the beginning of the piece consists of a stepwise descent of thirds in a high register. It is followed by a stepwise ascent of a lower melody, one moving more slowly. This up-and-down, wavelike motion of melodic material continues through much of the piece, but it is never exact or jerky. Rather, it is deployed loosely and with subtle variation, reminding us that no two waves are exactly the same.

The entire prelude, in fact, can be viewed as a giant wave with a smaller wave embedded within it. Consider that the overall ABA design is a type of a back-and-forth wave form. Within the first A section is a smaller aba wave, the smaller b subsection having the five-note turn that distinguishes the larger B section. (This type of foreshadowing is yet another hallmark of Debussy's style and was discussed earlier in chapter 3 in connection with *Pelléas et Mélisande*.) By combining the waves successively, an alternative overall pattern would be as follows:

A	B	A'	B'	A''
mm. 1–22	23–33	33–41	42–47	48–64

Most of us are probably unaware of these multiple layers of waves that comprise Debussy's *Voiles*, not just on the surface but beneath it as well. There is a kind of beauty in such complexity of form, which gives his music such impressive depth, vibrancy, and unity. Yet *Voiles* is a strange anomaly. It is the only Debussy work that is restricted to just two scales: the whole tone and the minor pentatonic. Given the limited harmonic palette he deliberately chose for this work, the result he achieved is a feat of ingenuity.

LA CATHÉDRALE ENGLOUTIE

Voiles was one of three piano preludes that Debussy created to evoke water. The other two are entitled *Ondine*, who was a beautiful water nymph in European mythology, and *La cathédrale engloutie*, which is based on another legend, the drowned city of Ys on the coast of Brittany. When the tide is low, the towers of the ancient Cathedral of Ys can be seen beneath the ocean surface, as if the magnificent structure is rising out of the waves. On occasion, the bells from the cathedral can still be heard ringing from the depths of the sea.

Debussy was not the first composer drawn to the ancient legend of Ys. That distinction belongs to the composer Edouard Lalo, the father of Debussy's friend Pierre Lalo. In 1875, Edouard wrote an opera entitled *Le roi d'Ys* (*The King of Ys*), an epic work that was only rarely performed during the twentieth century but is enjoying a revival in the twenty-first century, when complicated mythological shows like *Game of Thrones* are so popular. Debussy's setting of the Ys legend, by contrast, has long been one of his best-known works. He gave the premieres of "La cathédrale engloutie" and three other preludes—"Danseuses de Delphes," "Voiles," and "Danse de Puck"—on May 25, 1910.

It should be mentioned that Debussy's three water-inspired preludes are a subset of a larger category of piano preludes, namely, those that connect to nature. These are preludes that connect in various ways to the wind, the air, the sky, the seasons, and the weather. Together, his nature preludes constitute approximately half of the twenty-four preludes, a fact that testifies to Debussy's profound appreciation of the outdoors. Other, smaller categories of preludes are linked by common themes of antiquity, French poetry and culture, Spanish and American culture, and English literature. In a sense, the various categories of preludes listed here are a microcosm of the workings of Debussy's mind and compositional process. The same themes recur in his larger, more substantial works.

Debussy depicted the legend of the Cathedral of Ys via two main ideas, both of which are introduced at the beginning of the piece:

1. Slow-moving blocks of hollow chords (i.e., open fifths), which are spaced far apart and played very softly. They bring to mind the sound of church bells tolling in the distance.
2. Faster-moving chains of parallel-stacked chords with a steady rhythm and in an organum-like texture that evokes the religious ceremonies of medieval times.

Perhaps to underscore the religious aspect of this particular prelude, Debussy used an overall arch design:

A	B	C	B'	A'
mm. 1–27	28–46	47–41	72–83	84–89

A

The opening of the piece paints a picture of an old cathedral buried deep and unmoving in the water. By the middle of the first A section, we begin to hear a flowing triplet rhythm in a low register, our first indication that the dormant cathedral is stirring from the depths of its watery tomb. To draw the performer's attention to this important point, Debussy indicated *Peu à peu sortant de la brume* (Emerging from the fog little by little) at the top of the page. A few measures later, he added another marking, *Augmentez progressivement* (Slowly growing), and indeed we now hear even more rhythmic motion and activity. The volume has increased as well to *forte* and *più forte*, while the chantlike melody climbs to a higher register. All of these compositional elements work together to create the impression that the old cathedral is ascending higher and higher.

B

At the start of the B section, the cathedral breaks the surface with a powerful *fortissimimo* and with full and solid chords, which we might associate with blaring organ music. This is the loudest moment of the entire piece. The fact that Debussy selected C major as the key for this section is significant. Historically, composers used C major to symbolize majesty (Bach), victory (Beethoven), and celebration (Wagner). Debussy may have been aware of the inherent symbolism of the key since its appearance at this point in the piece is fitting. However, the victory celebration is short lived. After just five measures of C major, we hear first one extraneous pitch (B♭), followed by another one (A♭/G♯). These two altered pitches cloud the pure triumph of the moment. They also signal the strange and terrible time in the cathedral's past, which are about to be relayed in the central C section of the prelude.

C

The reason that the cathedral sank to the bottom of the ocean varies. Most versions of the Ys legend feature a fifth-century king named Gradlon and his daughter Dahut. The king was a good and pious man who held the key to the floodgate that protects the city. Dahut was a wicked princess. One night Princess Dahut stole the key and gave it to her lover, the devil. One of them opened the floodgate, and the city drowned.

In some ways, the middle C section of Debussy's prelude renders that particular moment in time, when disaster struck Ys. The section is in the key of C♯ minor, which not only jars with the preceding key of C major but also casts a blur. The dynamic levels contrast as well: here they are initially muffled and ghostly whereas the previous section was mostly loud and bright. Significantly, the tritone, or the interval of the augmented fourth, is articulated several times toward the end of the C section. The tritone was branded the *Diabolus in musica* (Devil in music) by medievalists. It was highly dissonant, and there were many treatises at that time that strictly forbade its use. However, many composers, especially those active in the nineteenth century, used the tritone to symbolize evil. Debussy was no exception. In his *La cathédrale engloutie*, he juxtaposes two tritones, F♯–C and G♯–D, at the end the section. They are isolated sounds emanating softly from a low register—a reminder that pure evil was at the root of the catastrophe that befell Ys.

B'

To be sure, the cathedral is sinking back beneath the surface of the water. While closely resembling the first B section in terms of material and key, the second B section sounds an octave lower, as if gravity is pulling down on the cathedral. Also telling are the low, rumbling arpeggios in the left-hand accompaniment, suggestive of air bubbles created by the sinking cathedral. The only extraneous pitch in this section is G♭, which is in a tritone relationship with the tonic key. The recurrence of the tritone here, when the end is near, is a last reminder of the role that evil played in the history of the Ys.

A'

The cathedral has completely disappeared and resettled at the bottom of the sea. Instead of rumbling arpeggios in the left-hand part, we hear sustained (i.e., motionless) pedal notes and chords. These are built on C1, the lowest pitch in the entire piece. While there is ascending motion in the middle and higher registers of the score, they impart a sense of dissolution, of the cathedral bells softly sounding and disappearing into thin air.

In many ways, "La cathédrale engloutie" and "Voiles" are very different depictions of water. This should come as no surprise given Debussy's stubborn refusal to duplicate compositional processes in his own music. The two works also give us some insight into his perception of the sea as constantly changing and capable of infinite variety. It could be motionless or flowing, familiar or strange, subtle or complex, and beautiful or frighteningly forceful.

But to paraphrase Pierre Boulez, the French conductor and composer, there seems to be a constant thread running through Debussy's music. In the case of *La cathédrale engloutie* and *Voiles*, that constant element is a type of foreshadowing whereby Debussy gives an early premonition of the center of a piece. Recall that in *Voiles*, which had an overall ABA design, a smaller aba wave was embedded in the opening A section, the small b subsection having the same five-note turn that distinguished the larger B section. Similarly, in *La cathédrale engloutie*, which follows an ABCB'A', the initial A section subdivides into an aca', with subsection c (mm. 7–13) anticipating the eerie C section. We will encounter this "wave within a wave" construction repeatedly in Debussy's work.

LA MER

Now that we have looked at two examples of Debussy's water music for piano, let us consider *La mer*, his most complex, concentrated, and majestic composition about the sea. All three movements (or symphonic sketches, to use his own words) are to be performed in sequence since they represent the course the sea can take during a single day. In "De l'aube à midi sur la mer" (From dawn to noon on the sea), the music emerges quietly out of the predawn darkness, as if it were awakening, blurry, and indistinct. Gradually, but not steadily, the motion quickens, the orchestral colors brighten, and the dynamic level increases. At the conclusion of this first sketch, a radiant brass chorale portrays the midday sun shining over the sea. "Jeux de vagues" ("Play of the Waves"), the second sketch, is a lively depiction of waves swaying and sparkling in the sunlight. Flashes of melody and ostinato patterns flit from section to section of the orchestra, sometimes overlapping and colliding with each other, as waves often do. In "Dialogue du vent et de la mer" (Dialogue of the wind and the sea), the third and final sketch, Debussy captures the intense interaction of two elemental forces. Like the first sketch, the third begins low and dark, but there is nothing relaxed or sleepy about the sea here. It sounds decisive and intense, full of menace. (To me, the opening and other passages in the third movement remind me of some of John Williams's iconic music for the movie *Jaws*.) At times, the music of the third sketch is calm, but the overall impression is of the sea gathering strength and volume from its interactions with the wind. The surge at the end of *La mer* is among the most powerful and thrilling music Debussy ever wrote.

La mer is one of those works that needs to be experienced live for full impact. Of course, some outstanding recordings do exist. Try Herbert von Karajan's 1964 recording, which is widely available. As you listen, do not try to find an explicit program along the lines of what Berlioz had written for his *Symphonie fantastique*. Debussy would never tell a straight story; the only explicit information he provides is the movement titles. Nor will you find tuneful melodies, conventional forms, or anything representational. Debussy's true aim in writing *La mer* was to convey how the sea makes us feel and how the sea is rich in complexity and nuance.

We can begin to understand *La mer* by recognizing a certain compositional procedure that Debussy uses in much of his other music. This is the process of duplication, whereby he presents a melodic idea or motif and then repeats it immediately—exactly or with minimal variation. Be aware, however, that the accompaniment may change at the repetition of the melody. As explained in chapter 3 and in connection with *Pelléas et Mélisande*, the effect of duplication is to give the listener the opportunity to slow down and savor the moment as well as the time to appreciate the changes of timbre, both subtle and dramatic, in the background. These changes will be almost nonstop; there is not even a pause between the first and second movements, and only a brief pause between the second and third. Just as the sea is ever moving, even when it is calm, so too is Debussy's *La mer*.

As well, notice how Debussy assigns roles to his instruments. The cellos, for instance, are sometimes used to suggest the depth of the ocean. At one point in the first movement, there are sixteen cellos playing. This is twice the number of cellos found in a standard orchestra and could be understood to represent the latent power that lies below the surface of the sea. Other instruments, such as the harps playing arpeggios in a high register, signify the rays of the sun.

As a means of demonstrating some of the structural innovations and intricacies of *La mer*, let us take a closer look at the first movement. From an overall perspective, "De l'aube à midi sur la mer" divides neatly into five sections due to clear changes in meter, tempo, key, and modality. These five sections are as follows:

Section	A	B	C	D	E
mm.	1–30	31–83	84–121	122–131	132–141

The above ABCDE design represents a considerable departure from textbook standards of musical form, which normally features a restatement of material. In effect, Debussy boldly dispensed with a recapitulation and instead created an open form. He activated the open-form process not only by omitting a recapitulation but also by presenting at least one new melodic motive in all but one of the five sections. Like the sea, the music he created is in a constant process of movement.

In the opening section, for instance, there are two new melodic motives distributed along a small-scale arch form, or abcba. At the center of the arch (c) is the first of two cyclic melodies that will recur in various guises later in the movement. It will also have a prominent role in the third movement. Sometimes labeled the "call of the sea," this cyclic melody is introduced softly by the English horn and a muted trumpet. It opens with repeated notes on middle C and then proceeds to trace two graceful waves. Framing the first cyclic theme are two statements of a shorter melodic motive (b), which is distinguished with a dotted rhythm and played both times by the solo oboe. Continuing outward, the outermost (a) passages have the same type of rocking motion provided by the two harps.

The one exception is the next-to-last section, (D), a scene lacking distinguishable melody and characterized by stillness and inactivity. No doubt, the introduction of a new motive here would be out of place. The timeless and mysterious quality of these ten measures may be due to the low Ab pedal point over which whole-tone and other dissonant harmonies seem to float in a beatless environment. Also strange is the pairing of a solo English horn with two solo cellos that occasionally venture into the higher end of their register. Together, these three instruments play a mostly whole-tone melodic line. At times, they combine to sound like a new and different single instrument.

A sense of quiet but impending power intensifies at the start of the fifth and final section of "De l'aube à midi sur la mer" as the trombones finally make their entrance. Softly, they join the other brass instruments in full triadic harmony—in essence, they play a chorale—from which the second cyclic melody emerges proudly and boldly. As mentioned above, the brass chorale captures the sun at high noon in blazing glory. Like the first cyclic motive, the second will later recur in the third movement.

One last piece of advice for experiencing *La mer*: Remember that Debussy had to find innovative ways of providing formal coherency and unity in this free-flowing, open-ended piece. One way he did this was by strategically replicating ideas on multiple levels of the structure. Consider, for instance, the successively larger surges he created at significant endings. There is a brief swell at the end of the A section of the first movement, a larger burst at the end of the first movement (i.e., the grand chorale), and then the massive surge at the conclusion of the third movement, with the entire orchestra playing at triple-*forte* in the final measures.

While the final surge is certainly the most impressive, the one culminating at the end of the first movement is perhaps more intriguing. In a sense, the triumphant chorale at the conclusion of the opening movement functions as an apotheosis that effectively replaces the traditional recapitulation. Creating an apotheosis instead of a recapitulation enabled Debussy to construct an open-ended form, a forward-looking design that was to be explored by later generations of composers.

AFTER THE PREMIERE OF *LA MER*

Debussy's *La mer* was performed for the first time on October 15, 1905, at the Concerts Lamoureux in Paris, with Camille Chevillard conducting. As usual, the initial reaction was mixed. Critics such as M. D. Calvocoressi praised Debussy's newest work, while others panned it. The cut that hurt Debussy the most came from a former supporter, Pierre Lalo, who quickly dismissed *La mer* as artificial. In his October 16, 1905, review in *Le Temps*, Lalo wrote,

It seems to me Debussy has willed himself to feel rather than really feeling deeply and naturally. For the first time, listening to a descriptive work by Debussy, I have the impression of standing, not in front of nature, but in front of a reproduction of nature; a wonderfully refined, ingenious and carefully composed reproduction, but a reproduction none the less . . . I do not hear, I do not see, I do not smell the sea.

Some members of the first audience were not inclined to accept *La mer* because of the composer's scandalous private life, which had reached the newspapers. According to his friend Louis Laloy (quoted in Edward Lockspeiser, *Debussy*), "The work was awaited in Paris with impatience that was not kindly disposed. Prudish indignation had not yet been appeased and on all sides people were ready to make the artist pay dearly for the wrongs that were imputed to the man." To be sure, the initial reception of *La mer* marked the beginning of a low point in Debussy's reputation. When the next performances of *La mer* took place, in the United States in 1907, critical reaction was again mixed and mostly unfavorable. Said Louis C. Elson, the music critic for the *Boston Daily Advertiser*, on April 22, 1907,

It is possible that Debussy did not intend to call it "La mer," but "Le Mal de Mer," which would at once make the tone-picture as clear as day. It is a series of symphonic pictures of seasickness. The first movement is Headache. The second is Doubt, picturing moments of dread suspense. . . . The third movement, with its explosions and rumblings, has now a self-evident purpose: The hero is endeavoring to throw up his boot heels!

Nor did the New York press mince any words. The following is an extract of a review that appeared in the *New York Post* on March 22, 1907,

The Sea of Debussy does not call for many words of comment. The three parts of which it is composed are entitled *From Dawn till Noon*, *Play of the Waves*, and *Dialogue of the Wind and the Sea*, but as far as any pictorial suggestiveness is concerned, they might as well have been entitled *On the Flatiron Building*, *Slumming in the Bowery*, and *A Glimpse of Chinatown during a Raid*. Debussy's music is the dreariest kind of rubbish. Does anybody for a moment doubt that

> Debussy would not write such chaotic, meaningless, cacophonous, ungrammatical stuff, if he could invent a melody? . . . Even his orchestration is not particularly remarkable.

In Debussy's private life, however, October 1905 would prove to be a time of some positive changes. Days before the premiere of *La mer*, he and Emma Bardac moved into an elegant townhouse at 64 avenue du Bois de Boulogne (now 80 avenue Foch), one of the most expensive residential areas in the world. The rent alone cost ten thousand francs a year, paid by Emma with the pension she received from her ex-husband, a wealthy banker. Erik Satie, Debussy's longtime friend from the Montmartre days, rightly described the townhouse as sumptuous. Then, two weeks after the premiere, Emma gave birth to Chouchou, who would prove to be a source of inspiration for many of Debussy's works, including the 1908 *Children's Corner*. She was also a source of joy unlike any other. In a letter to Louis Laloy dated November 4, 1905, written shortly after Chouchou's birth, Debussy stated, "I have been, for a few days, the father of a little girl—the joy of which has upset me and leaves me a bit frightened" (Debussy, *Correspondance* [1872–1918], 929).

As for *La mer*, it overcame the sting of initial opposition and turned into one of Debussy's most popular works. One of the first conductors to champion *La mer* and whose performances and recordings helped to smooth the way for wider acceptance was Arturo Toscanini. He first conducted the piece in 1909 in Milan. After the war, *La mer* became a showpiece of his repertoire. In the United States alone, he conducted thirty-two performances of the work with the New York Philharmonic, eighteen with the NBC Symphony Orchestra, and three with the Philadelphia Orchestra. The two studio recordings he made were with the Philadelphia Orchestra in 1942 and with the NBC Symphony Orchestra in 1950.

6

A FRENCH NATIONALIST WITH AN EYE
TOWARD THE EAST

In June and July of 1889, a young Claude Debussy attended the Exposition Universelle, a world's fair held in Paris that year and attended by over thirty million people. This magnificent event featured eighteen pavilions representing French colonies and thirty-one pavilions showcasing other cultures around the world. These included Algeria, Argentina, Bolivia, Chile, Gabon, Hawaii, Mexico, Nicaragua, Tonkin, and Tunisia.

The success of the exposition demonstrated the breadth of interest that Europeans had in foreign cultures. Composers were especially drawn to the completely new sounds and musical forms, and they quickly incorporated them into their own music. It was there that the young Debussy encountered the Javanese gamelan orchestra and Annamite (Vietnamese) theater. For some writers, his prominent use of pentatonic scales was inspired by the five-note *slendro* from Java. His fondness for static devices, such as the ostinatos and unchanging pedal points in *Pagodes* (1903), might also be traced to gamelan music.

Debussy's fascination with the arts of other cultures would recur throughout his life. As mentioned in the preceding chapter, he hung a copy of Hokusai's iconic *Great Wave off Kanogawa* on his office wall. Another item from his office, a Japanese lacquer cabinet depicting koi carp, was the inspiration behind the title of "Poissons d'or," the final movement of *Images*, book 2, for piano (1907). He evoked ancient Greece in two piano preludes, "Danseuses de Delphes" (1910) and

"Canope" (1913); *Syrinx* for solo flute (1913); and, of course, *Prelude to "The Afternoon of a Faun."* He evoked England in the "Hommage à S. Pickwick Esq. P.P.M.P.C.," which begins with a quotation of the British national anthem in the bass line. The title of this prelude (from book 2) is a reference to the main character of Charles Dickens's first novel, *The Posthumous Papers of the Pickwick Club* (or *The Pickwick Papers*).

Debussy also drew ideas from American culture in "Golliwog's Cakewalk," the sixth and final movement of *Children's Corner*. The two title elements refer to a popular minstrel doll named Golliwog, which Chouchou owned, and a mid-nineteenth-century dance performed by black American slaves on Southern plantations. The winner of the cakewalk competition would receive a cake for a prize. The music for a cakewalk was ragtime, which Debussy had heard in the music halls of Montmartre. In keeping with the ragtime style, "Golliwog's Cakewalk" has a four-bar introduction on the dominant and a 2/4 time signature. The piece also features the idiosyncratic rhythm of ragtime: steady, marchlike rhythms played staccato by the left hand on the piano and syncopated—or ragged—rhythms by the right hand. As mentioned in chapters 1 and 4, other compositions by Debussy were influenced by the sounds of Russia and Spain.

Debussy's wide-ranging interest in the visual, decorative, and musical arts of other cultures indicates openness, an appreciation of difference, and curiosity. Throughout his creative life, he would explore new timbres and technical possibilities. But first and foremost, he was a proud Frenchman. Nowhere is this more evident than in his last works.

THE WARTIME WORKS

The compositions Debussy composed between 1914 and 1918 were prompted by the impact of World War I. A fervent patriot, he believed that the war against Germany could be fought not only on the battlefield but through music as well. "Do not our soldiers, who trudge heroically through the mud singing songs in which sheer rhythm trumps over good taste, have the right to shrug their shoulders at our [French musicians'] futile preoccupation? Let us hope that they will forgive us and will realize that there are many paths to victory! Music, fertile and admirable, is one of them" (*DOM*, 325). Not surprisingly, many of his wartime compositions commemorate French allies, composers, or soldiers. In a sense, they may be regarded as part of Debussy's contribution to the war effort. In 1914 he wrote *Berceuse héroïque*, which he dedicated to King Albert I of Belgium and his soldiers. It was the only composition he completed during the first year of the war since he was so depressed about the German invasion. The following year saw the composition of three works: the *Douze Etudes*, dedicated to the memory of Frédéric Chopin; the second movement of *En blanc et noir* (1915), dedicated to Jacques Charlot, Debussy's friend, who was killed in action; and the *Noël des enfants qui n'ont plus de maison* (1915) for homeless refugee children in Flanders. He also began a series of six sonatas for various combinations of instruments, taking as a point of departure the aesthetics of the French masters of the eighteenth century. Finally in 1916, stricken with cancer, he started but did not complete his last work, the *Ode à la France* for solo voice (depicting Joan of Arc), chorus (by turns the voice of heaven and earth), and orchestra.

The extent to which Debussy aimed to express his patriotic sentiments in musical terms varies in these works. To consider briefly a well-known example, the second movement of *En blanc et noir* is a vivid musical portrayal of the war waged between Germany and France. In this two-piano work, Debussy juxtaposed a clumsy, discordant setting of the Lutheran chorale *Ein Festburg*, here obviously signifying the German invaders, with a light, delicate French tune. Toward the end of the movement, faint strains of the *Marseillaise* are heard, an indication of his hope for an ultimate French victory as well as his firm belief in the endurance of French art.

From the perspective of Debussy's entire output, his late works are a final testament to his long-standing obsession to escape the immediate past. One musical example that immediately comes to mind is "Hommage à Rameau," the second piece in the first book of *Images* for piano composed in 1904–1905. In addition to setting poems and texts by his contemporaries like Verlaine, Mallarmé, and Maeterlinck, he set poems by the medieval French poet François Villon in 1908, and the first and third pieces of *Three Songs of France* (1904). His interest in the French musical tradition can also be seen in his editorial work for Durand. Debussy, d'Indy, Saint-Saëns, Ravel, and Dukas were among the principle collaborators of the Rameau Classic Edition published by Durand

and begun in 1894. For his part, Debussy revised and arranged for piano Jean-Philippe Rameau's *Les Fêtes de Polymnie.*

Because Debussy's interest in pre-romantic French music and literature extended throughout much of his career, broad descriptive labels such as "neoclassic," "nationalistic," and "patriotic" are inaccurate and misleading terms when exclusively applied to the late works. Quite simply, there was no great shift in Debussy's thought, only a more concentrated and intensified effort during the war. He reaffirmed his unwavering commitment to a national French art in an article entitled "Alone at Last! . . ." that appeared in the March 11, 195 issue of *L'Intransigeant.* The article's main intent is a sharp rebuke against both his French predecessors and contemporaries for embracing the heavy, opulent music of Germany at the expense of the "light and clear" French art:

> For many years now I have been saying the same thing: that we have been unfaithful to the musical traditions of our own race for more than a century and a half.
>
> It is true that the public have often been misled because they have been presented with the latest fashion as if it were part of a purely French tradition. We have obscured the roots of our music's family tree: the careless observer has seen only parasitic creepers, and our indulgence toward the naturalized has been limitless!
>
> In fact, since Rameau, we have had no purely French tradition. His death severed the thread, Ariadne's thread, that guided us through the labyrinth of the past. Since then, we have failed to cultivate our garden, but on the other hand we have given a warm welcome to any foreign salesmen who cared to come our way. We listened to their patter and bought their worthless wares, and when they laughed at our ways we became ashamed of them. We begged forgiveness of the muses of good taste for having been so light and clear, and we intoned a hymn to the praise of heaviness. We adopted ways of writing that were quite contrary to our nature, and excesses of language far from compatible with our own ways of thinking. We tolerated overblown orchestras, tortuous forms, cheap luxury and clashing colors, and we were about to give the seal of approval to even more suspect naturalizations when the sound of gunfire put a sudden stop to it all.

Despite the simplification of material in Debussy's wartime works, in no sense are they an abdication to a more conventionally oriented conception. On the contrary, Debussy blends in a completely personal manner the retrogressive aspects with the truly innovative. Considered in this way, his late works renew, and hence transform, the classical source.

THE SIX SONATAS

The different positions of the dates on the autograph manuscript of the first sonata, the Sonata for Cello and Piano, suggest that this work was begun and completed during the summer of 1915. "Eté 1915 = Cl. Debussy" is inscribed in Debussy's hand on the title page as well as the end of the manuscript.

It is possible that he had in mind a general plan of the entire project as well as the instrumentation of all six sonatas when he began work on the Cello Sonata. The general nature of the series is first described by Debussy in a letter to the Italian conductor Bernardo Molinari on October 6, 1915:

> I haven't written much orchestral music, but I have finished: Douze Etudes for piano, a Cello Sonata, another Sonata for Flute, Viola, and Harp, in the ancient, flexible mould with none of the grandiloquence of modern sonatas. There are going to be six of them for different groups of instruments and the last one will combine all those used in the previous five. For many people, that won't be as important as an opera. . . . But I thought it was of greater service to music!

A more detailed plan of the instrumentation for the six sonatas comes from an undated, single sheet of notepaper housed in the Bibliothèque Nationale in Paris. It tells us that the third sonata was initially conceived as not only a trio for violin, English horn, and piano (the definite version is a duo for violin and piano) but also the instrumentation for the remaining three sonatas. The fourth was to have been for oboe, horn, and harpsichord; the fifth for trumpet, clarinet, bassoon, and piano; and the sixth in the form of a "concert" that would have combined the double bass with all the different instruments used in the previous sonatas.

In his late sonatas, Debussy commemorated the French musical heritage by resurrecting the aesthetics of eighteenth-century French masters like François Couperin and Jean-Philippe Rameau, whom he considered France's last great composers. Debussy held that ever since Rameau, the true French musical traditional was overshadowed, if not squelched, by a continuous parade of foreign composers, with the result that France no longer had its own traditional:

> The reason why French music forgot about Rameau for half a century [probably a century and a half] is one of those mysteries so common in the history of art. It can, perhaps, be explained only by a fortuitous series of historical events. The queen, Marie Antoinette, an Austrian through and through (something for which she had to pay in the end), imposed Gluck upon the French taste; as a result our traditions were led astray, our desire for clarity drowned, and having gone through Meyerbeer, we ended up, naturally enough, with Richard Wagner. But why? Wagner was necessary for a blossoming of the art in Germany—a prodigious blossoming, although, in the end, virtually funeral—but it would not be unusual to doubt that he could ever have any success in France, and influence our way of thing so much. If it is only the future that can these things into perspective objectively, we must at least be certain of one hard fact: that there is no longer a French tradition. (*DOM*, 229)

Concerning the sonatas' resemblance to the actual musical practices of early French masters, the first movement of the Cello Sonata and the second movement of the Trio relate specifically to Rameau's opera *Les Fêtes de Polymnie*, which Debussy had edited several years earlier for Durand. Yet the sonatas are also based on a synthesis of French musical classicism and the sonatas of eighteenth-century central European artists like J. S. Bach and Arcangelo Corelli. In other words, they derive from an international eighteenth-century style.

Thus, the antiquated rondeau in the third movement of the Violin Sonata is loosely modeled on rondeaus such as those found in the orders of Couperin's *Pièces de clavecin* and the keyboard suites of Rameau. By contrast, the grouping of the series into six sonatas and the three-movement plans for each of the sonatas follow the sonatas and concertos of Bach and Corelli. Even the title page that prefaces each Debussy sonata—"Six Sonates / Pour divers instruments / Composée par / Claude Debussy / Musicien Français"—resembles the printed title pages of works like Bach's *Musical Offering*, rather than of French publications. Some elements common to both French and non-French sources include the Italian dance title, Tempo di minuetto, for the second movement of the Trio Sonata; the large-scale sequence in the first movement of the Violin Sonata; and points of imitation, plagal cadences, and improvisational qualities. As well, there is a common key for the movements of each sonata. All three movements of the Trio Sonata are rooted in F: the first movement is in F major, the second in F minor, and the third begins in F minor and concludes in F major. In the Violin Sonata, the first movement is rooted in G minor and the second and third are in G major. In the Cello Sonata, the first movement begins in D minor and concludes in D major, while the third movement is in D minor. There is no tonic reference point in the second movement of the Cello Sonata, but the key signature of D minor is indicated.

These and other old-fashioned elements of style are no more than a veneer of the older style. Debussy's true homage to his French heritage in the late sonatas can be found in their diminutive proportions, small and intimate instrumental ensembles, clear formal schemes, and light and transparent textures. It was this marked simplification and clarity of material that Debussy considered to be the essence of French classical art and the antithesis of the huge orchestras, complicated forms, and massive sound of Wagner, Beethoven, and other romantic composers. With regard to the Cello Sonata, for example, he once wrote, "It's not for me to judge its excellence but I like its proportions and its almost classical form, in the good sense of the word" (*Letters*, 299). Thus, his aesthetics can be understood as a twofold negative reaction: to foreign (i.e., German) works in particular and, like other early twentieth-century works, to musical romanticism in general.

A CLOSER LOOK: FIRST MOVEMENT OF THE CELLO SONATA

The "Prologue" (first movement) of Debussy's Cello Sonata, the first entry in the proposed set of six sonatas, successfully resurrects a preromantic style in a number of ways. In direct contrast to the huge, sprawling designs of some nineteenth-century music, the overall shape of the first movement is compact, spanning a length of only fifty-one measures. Compared to some of his more tonally adventurous works where dissonant sonorities act as stable points of arrival, the movement's referential feature is the triad, appearing clearly and unambiguously at strong focal points. Still other explicit references to an older musical style exist: a transparent and slender texture, occasional well-defined phrases, plagal cadences, and modal allusions. The main impression, especially at the outset of the work, is one of simplicity, clarity, and restraint. As for the overall design, it may be heard as a three-part ABA' form, preceded by a short piano introduction:

Section	Introduction	A	B	A'
mm.	1–7	8–15	16–38	39–51

The movement's form is hardly as unpretentious or stagnant as an ABA' label might suggest. To be sure, this simple description masks the modern path Debussy was taking at the time. In brief, the structure of the movement evolves from a retro style (introduction and A section) to a much more progressive procedure involving intervals and cells (B section), and then back to the retrogressive sound (A' section).

The introduction begins with a clear and strong (*forte*) tonic chord on the downbeat of measure 1. There is no ambiguity whatsoever, unlike the beginning of the *Prelude to "The Afternoon of a Faun."* The next harmonies are also straightforward and diatonic in that there are no altered or chromatic pitches, just pure and simple sounds, with occasional allusions to the ancient minor-like Dorian mode. As well, the phrase structure in the opening measures is quite clear, consisting of two two-measure subphrases, and then follows an example of *style brisé*. These are the arpeggiated chords in the piano part that give the impression of French lute music.

When the cello enters in the introductory section, the well-defined phrase structure breaks down into a free improvisation based on the preceding measures. Essentially, the cello enters with a cadenza, as in Brahms's Double Concerto (op. 102) and many of Liszt's and Saint-Saëns's concertos. This extreme contrast produces an effect of suspended time and is accompanied by a key change, chromatic harmonies, and asymmetrical phrasing.

Let's move ahead to the body of the movement, where the cellular process is activated. This highly innovative technique may be best described as a progressive expansion and contraction of musical intervals. It is a kind of growth and decay process, whereby an interval and its symmetrical inverse (e.g., minor third-major sixth) characterize or govern a specific area of the piece. The progression is by semitone. At first, intervals expand: minor and major seconds are embedded within the opening A section, minor and major thirds are emphasized at the start of the B section, and perfect fourth-perfect fifth sets dominate the middle of the B section. In the second half of the piece, by contrast, the intervallic process reverses: cells begin to contract to major and minor thirds in the latter half of B, and then to major and minor seconds at the end of B and beginning of A'. As you listen to a recording of the work, the intervallic process is not completely obvious, but you will certainly hear multiple perfect fourths and fifths marked *largement déclamé* in the middle of the movement. Played *forte* in the key of C major, these largest intervals serve as the midpoint of the entire interval process as well as the climax of the movement.

The final section of the movement, A', is a true reprise featuring a literal restatement of the main theme from A. The repeat of original material is brief, however, and is limited to only four measures. The remaining measures of A' contrast with the original A and combine material from both the introduction and opening A sections. The movement concludes with a Picardy third, a chord with a raised or major third, which French composers like Couperin used to end their minor key compositions. The appearance of the triad here is Debussy's final allusion to a pre-romantic musical style.

To summarize, in the first movement of his Cello Sonata, Debussy utilized aspects of an older musical style in conjunction with a highly innovative intervallic technique. (This is not to say that the cellular process in the Cello Sonata represents a brand new approach for Debussy. A few writers have identified similar structures in even earlier Debussy works, such as *La mer*.) The highest concentration of anachronistic elements occurs in the outer A and introductory sections. These elements include the *style brisé* in the piano part of the introduction, modal allusions, and a Picardy third to close the movement. The cellular aspect of the piece invites comparison with the theory and music of one of Debussy's contemporaries, Arnold Schoenberg. What distinguishes him from Schoenberg and other Viennese atonal composers of the time is this: Debussy never completely rejected the underlying tonality or modality of a piece. Unlike his Viennese contemporaries, he was not as radical, preferring instead to explore new sounds and structures and push boundaries from within a tonal or modal framework.

A LIFE INTERRUPTED

None of the last three sonatas was realized. Less than two months after his October 15, 1915, letter to Molinari, Debussy underwent surgery on December 7, 1915, for rectal cancer, a disease that had plagued him for several years but had now reached an advanced stage. Then followed a six-month period of depression and tremendous suffering, with frequent administrations of radium and morphine. Needless to say, his creative work came to a standstill. His letters during this period are a moving document of the unbearable pain and frustration caused by his inability to work. He wrote to Robert Godet, a longtime friend, on February 4, 1916: "I've just started a new treatment. It's all shrouded in mystery and I'm asked to be patient. . . . Good God! Where am I to find patience? After sixty days of various tortures." Four months later on June 5, 1916, he wrote to Victor Segalen, another friend of long standing: "Without realizing it, I've spent a full six months now contemplating my misery; it's too long for someone who hasn't the time to lose any more. Will I ever again know what it is to be well? I don't dare to think so and I'd much rather have a sudden end than this pursuit of health in which, so far, the disease is always one step ahead of me." During the late spring and summer of 1916, Debussy's health improved somewhat, and with stoic determination he decided to return to work. On July 3, 1916, he wrote to his editor Jacques Durand: "I am not well enough to affirm this, but I have decided to go on, to work and no longer be under the orders of an illness a little too bossy! We'll see. If I should disappear shortly, I want, at least, to have tried to do my duty."

Understandably, only two new compositions were begun in 1916. He sketched, but did not complete, *Ode à la France* for solo voice, chorus, and orchestra. He also completed the first movement of the Violin Sonata and had hoped to complete the remaining two movements, but he had much difficulty completing the third and final movement. Altogether, there were six versions of the movement, which Debussy called "this terrible finale." It was not until April 1917 that he finished the definitive version of the finale.

The Violin Sonata was Debussy's last completed work. It received its premiere at a benefit for blind war veterans at the Salle Gaveau, with Gaston Poulet and Debussy performing, on May 5, 1917. It was his last public performance. Less than a year later, on March 25, 1918, Debussy was dead at the age of fifty-five. His funeral took place on March 28, and he was buried in Père Lachaise cemetery.

In 1919 his body was reinterred in the Passy Cemetery. That same year, Chouchou Debussy died at age thirteen during the diphtheria epidemic. Both Chouchou and her mother Emma, who died in 1934, are buried with Debussy.

Upon visiting Passy, visitors are sometimes surprised to learn that Debussy's gravestone is so simple and understated. Their reaction is understandable. After all, he was and continues to be the greatest composer France has ever produced. The inscription reads as follows:

Claude Debussy

Musicien Français

August 22, 1862—March 25, 1918

His daughter and his wife are with him

Given Debussy's refined aesthetics and proud nationalist spirit, the inscription is right and fitting.

7

DEBUSSY'S ACHIEVEMENT AND LEGACY

Because 2018 marked the centennial of the death of Claude Debussy, France's greatest composer, more attention than usual was focused on him. Scholars from around the world did their part by convening at several European universities to reflect on Debussy, to celebrate his achievement, and to present new research on the man and his music. One conference, Claude Debussy in 2018: A Centenary Celebration, had a two-part, back-to-back structure and took place in late March 2018. The first part of the conference, Debussy Perspectives, 1918–2018, was at the Royal Northern College of Music in Manchester, England. At the conclusion of the Manchester sessions, the Debussy scholars boarded a motor coach for a three-hour trip to the University of Glasgow in Scotland. This second part of the conference was entitled Debussy's Late Work and the Musical Worlds of Wartime Paris. The final chamber concert in Glasgow featured his three late sonatas alongside new compositions inspired by Debussy and scored for the three ensembles (out of the projected six) he did not live to complete.

The worldwide centennial celebrations have intensified interest in Debussy and his body of work. Some, like the conferences in England and Scotland, are designed to enrich our understanding of him. But in the end, we will still be unable to completely understand his music. This may be because Debussy is full of extreme contradictions.

On the one hand, we have a rebel who cultivated a position as a revolutionary and nonconformist. Even before he became famous, he was not afraid to stand up to authority. In 1901, a year before the scandalous premiere of *Pelléas et Mélisande*, he wrote a critique wherein his oppositional attitude comes through loud and clear: "He [Mussorgsky] is quite unique, and will be renowned for an art that suffers from no stultifying rules or artificialities. . . . There is no question of any such thing as 'form,' or, at least, any forms there are have such complexity that they are impossible to relate to the accepted form—the 'official' ones" (*DOM*, 20–21).

On the other hand, he was an insider who knew what it took to get ahead in life. He gained acceptance to the Paris Conservatory. He competed and won the prestigious Rome Prize. He joined the National Society of Music, often regarded as a conservative bastion, but one that allowed performances of more unusual works, such as Debussy's String Quartet. Nor in his music did he ever choose to completely overturn tradition. Rather, in works such as the Cello Sonata, he resurrected the ancient Greek modes and combined them with the intervallic and cellular techniques associated with Schoenberg, usually regarded as a much more radical composer. This French rebel found a way to thrive within the classical tradition.

On the one hand, we have a composer whose works are often pegged as the musical equivalent of Impressionism. The implication is that his main focus was on floating sonorities, hazy outlines, and shimmering colors. On the other hand, beneath the free- and spontaneous-sounding surface of his music was a foundation that was carefully crafted and well constructed. His manuscript scores give evidence of his attention toward refinement of detail and a tendency for constant revision. In addition, there are numerous accounts of his home office on the Avenue du Bois du Boulogne, all testifying to Debussy's obsessive neatness and his penchant for precision and perfection. There was nothing out of place. According to his stepdaughter Dolly Bardac (as quoted in Roger Nichols, *Debussy Remembered*, 1992),

> He was very slow in his movements, very meticulous in himself and with everything that surrounded him. The objects of his worktable were arranged in an order which never changed. He was never parted from a big wooden toad, a Chinese ornament called Arkël which was on his table; he even took it travelling with him. With regard to this I found a piece of paper on which Debussy had clearly written at the moment of departure: "Do not put Arkël in the trunk; he doesn't like that."

We have Debussy the pop composer, whose "Clair de Lune" and other music live on in movie soundtracks, as well as the Debussy whose complex music has long vexed scholars. Rarely do two analyses of a single Debussy work agree completely. We have Debussy the Bohemian frequenting the cabarets and cafés of Montmartre with his friend Erik Satie, and the Debussy sharing the more rarefied, brainy atmosphere of Mallarmé's famous Tuesday evening receptions, a hub of Parisian intellectual life. In attendance were the leading figures of literature, painting, and sculpture.

We have a composer, able to draw from different music styles from across the world, including German, Russian, Javanese, Austrian, and American. But never did he forget his French heritage, especially during the First World War, when his long-standing patriotic sentiments were at the fore. If he had lived longer, we can only wonder what his next three sonatas would have been like, not to mention other types of music. At the time of his death in 1918, he still had so much more to give.

The complexity and eclecticism of his work help to explain why Debussy still fascinates us today. Another reason is the inherent freedom of his music. For Motoo Ôtaguro (1893–1979), Japan's first music critic, Debussy's music was emotional, freeing, and like the sea. The piece that drew me to Debussy's music was "Nuages" (Clouds), the opening movement of the *Nocturnes* (1899). I first heard it as a freshman in college in a music history course on twentieth-century music; the other assigned listening materials included Stravinsky's *Firebird*, Schoenberg's *Pierrot Lunaire*, Berg's *Wozzeck*, and Milhaud's *Le boeuf sur le toit* (The Ox on the Roof or The Nothing-Doing Bar). Of all these and other compositions I heard that semester, it was the Debussy that I found most intriguing. I would go to the listening lab in the library and play a 33 LP recording of just "Nuages" repeatedly throughout the semester. I found it comforting and relaxing. I felt both cocooned and freed at the same time. Today, as I near the last decade of my professional career, I am still finding new things in Debussy's music, such as the rhythmic and timbral complexities of *Jeux*, the last orchestral work he began in August 1912 and completed in late April 1913. The premiere, danced by Sergei Diaghilev's Ballets Russes, took place on May 15, 1913, at the Théâtre des Champs-Elysées, with Pierre Monteux conducting.

JEUX

By all accounts, Debussy's inspiration for *Jeux* (as well as for some of his other compositions) was stimulated by his need for money. At the time, he was continuing to live well beyond his means with his wife Emma and their daughter Chouchou in a rented townhouse on the upscale avenue du Bois de Boulogne. He was also in ill health and in debt to his publisher Jacques Durand and his friend Louis Laloy. Debussy's first response, sent by telegram to Diaghilev, the Russian ballet impresario, was outright negative. As stated in the 1949 memoir *La Pêche aux souvenirs* by Jacques-Emile Blanche, one of the sponsors of Diaghilev's ballets, Debussy's telegram read, "Subject ballet *Jeux* idiotic, not interested." When Diaghilev doubled his original offer to ten thousand French francs, Debussy reconsidered and agreed to write the music for the innovative ballet that Diaghilev had in mind. This sum would more than cover the annual rent of Debussy's posh home, which was set at ten thousand francs.

Jeux was not Debussy's first ballet. In 1910 he had accepted a commission from the Canadian-born dancer Maud Allan for *Isis*, later renamed *Khamma*. Although he had completed a piano reduction of *Khamma* in 1912, the stubborn Debussy and the equally stubborn Allan reached an artistic impasse and they parted ways; the orchestration was later completed by Charles Koechlin. Also in 1912, Debussy agreed to allow the twenty-two-year-old Vaslav Nijinsky, already a living legend in the world of dance, to choreograph *The Afternoon of a Faun* for Diaghilev's Ballets Russes. Once again, the respective views of the composer and lead dancer did not go in the same direction. Whereas Debussy's music was all about subtlety and beauty, Nijinsky's premiere performance in the title role was so sexually explicit that *Le Figaro* labeled the production as obscene. The second performance, attended by members of the French police, was sold out. Debussy himself was highly critical of Nijinsky's choreography and kept his distance. "Faun," Debussy said, "you are ugly. Go away!" (quoted in Lockspeiser, *Debussy*, 1978).

In light of Debussy's flawed collaborations with such cutting-edge choreographers as Maud Allan and Vaslav Nijinsky, we can understand why Debussy's initial reaction to Diaghilev's *Jeux* in the summer of 1912 was a blunt refusal. It is fortunate that Debussy changed his mind and accepted Diaghilev's offer since the musical score for *Jeux* is now regarded as one of the composer's most brilliant and prophetic works.

The Scenario

The scenario of *Jeux* was risqué for the time. According to Nijinsky's diaries, he and Diaghilev developed the story together. Originally, Diaghilev wanted to portray an erotic encounter among three men, and Nijinsky suggested the addition of a crashing airplane to the plot. In the end, they settled on a story about a three-way tennis game between a man and two women, with the women attracted to each other as well as to the man. The title itself—*Play*—can point toward sports or play.

Jeux begins at dusk, in an empty park, into which a tennis ball bounces. Under the glow of electric lights, a young man, followed by the two women, enter the scene and look for the ball. Although all three are dressed in white tennis clothes, they never actually play a game of tennis. Rather, during the next seventeen minutes, they flirt, show off, quarrel, sulk, and demonstrate just how capricious courtship can be. In the penultimate scene, the dancers reconcile and waltz together, their limbs interwoven. Their dance concludes with a three-way kiss that "binds them in ecstasy." This is the climax of the entire ballet, but then another tennis ball is thrown by an unknown hand and lands nearby. This time, the surprise appearance of the tennis ball seems to be menacing, rather than an impetus to more fun and games. Startled and afraid, the dancers scatter in different directions into the shadowy park.

Created on the eve of World War I, *Jeux* presents a story of young people frolicking and experimenting—a last dance, if you will. There is, however, a dark undertone throughout the story that becomes more pronounced by the end. When I saw a performance of *Jeux* a few months ago, the tennis ball that mysteriously flies in the dancers' midst at the end of the ballet reminded me of a grenade.

A Ballet Flop

For many musicians, *Jeux* has an affinity to one of Debussy's earlier works, the *Prelude to "The Afternoon of a Faun."* Pierre Boulez, for instance, summarized *Jeux* as The Afternoon of a Faun in sports clothes." In terms of narrative, Boulez's words ring true. Common elements include the theme of pursuit and the implied ménage à trois of one man and two women. In addition, the young man is a voyeur who spies on the young women. Other writers see musical connections between both orchestral works as well, but I find the distinguishing features of *Jeux* to be more fascinating. They point to a new path Debussy was following toward the end of his life, a path only recognized and applauded after his death by younger generations of composers. In 1913, however, his music for *Jeux* was not fully appreciated.

I can think of at least two reasons why the music of *Jeux* was initially ignored. First, during the initial performances in May 1913, Debussy's music was almost eclipsed by Nijinsky's radical style of choreography and, as was the case with their previous collaboration in 1912, their artistic visions clashed. Nijinsky and the other two dancers often moved mechanically, in a "marionette" style. They had a stiff posture, with elbows and wrists lightly bent and angled, and hands balled into fists. They positioned themselves so that their heads faced one way and their hips another. Clearly, this was no traditional ballet. While Pierre Lalo and other journalists quickly praised the "subtle" music of *Jeux*, they could not help but point out the unfortunate disparity between Debussy's delicate music and Nijinsky's disjointed dance style.

Then, barely two weeks after the premiere, there was another new ballet from the Ballets Russes. This was *The Rite of Spring*, which opened on May 29, 1913, also at the Théâtre des Champs-Elysées. The brutal force of Igor Stravinsky's music, combined with Nijinsky's bizarre choreography of stomping steps and a strange story of pagan sacrifice, appalled Parisian theatergoers. They were booing and hissing from the first bars of piece. When the curtain rose and the dancers appeared, the audience protested even more loudly and vigorously, to such an extent that the music could not be heard. A riot ensued, with members of the audience attacking each other and throwing vegetables at the orchestra. Reportedly, forty people were ejected at the debut performance. The scandal surrounding the launch of *The Rite of Spring* helped to make this newest ballet by Diaghilev a massive hit, one that fully eclipsed any impact that the much more understated *Jeux* might have had. Put simply, *Jeux* was a flop, at least in 1913.

Additionally, most members of the first audiences found the music of *Jeux* to be enigmatic and inaccessible. Even today, when listening to it, your initial impression may well be one of confusion. There are no long melodies, recurring motives, clear tonal centers, or other musical signposts resonating through the score. Rather, as explained by critic Emile Vuillermoz (and as quoted in Léon Vallas, *Claude Debussy: His Life and Works*, 1933), the music "changes speed and nuance every two measures; it abandons a figure, a timbre, a gesture, in order to go headlong in another direction." Indeed, there are more than sixty tempo markings within a time span of eighteen minutes. The overall quick pace enhances the fleeting quality of the music, as does the lack of a strong tonic key, which past composers used to anchor their works. One writer estimates that the tonic key of *Jeux* (A major) only appears in 42 of the total 709 measures. Sometimes, recognizable dances such as the old-fashioned waltz do emerge from the stream of material. These dances are brief and kept to a minimum so that the overall sense of quick and constant change is not impeded for long. While it is daunting to track the multiple ideas in *Jeux* (there are a total of twenty-three themes, according to one writer), the near constant rush of ideas in the music perfectly complements the story line of energetic young people in a mode of playful experimentation.

Before concentrating on selected passages of *Jeux*, I digress for a moment to offer an explanation about the appearance of old-fashioned dances in this modern ballet. We might think of a waltz in a Debussy work as a curious throwback, but his decision to include this dance was both deliberate and progressive for the time. Often the term *neoclassicism* can be understood as a trend dating from the 1920s and associated with Stravinsky. But retro styles, forms, and genres—in combination with new ideas—had already appeared in the music of Debussy, Ravel, Schoenberg, and other innovative composers of the time. In truth, the term neoclassicism is misleading. Consider just two examples that predate Stravinsky's so-called neoclassical period: (1) Ravel's *Le Tombeau de Couperin* (1917) for piano, a six-movement suite of mostly Baroque dances and forms (rigaudon, minuet, toccata, and others); and (2) Schoenberg's *Pierrot lunaire* (1912), which utilizes a fugue ("Der Mondflect"), a passacaglia ("Nacht"), and other Baroque techniques. In addition, and as mentioned in the preceding chapter, Debussy continued to follow the neoclassic trend for the remainder of his life. His last works included the three sonatas through which he sought to capture "la musique classique française" of the eighteenth century.

The Music

Although the music of *Jeux* can be appreciated independently, it can also be enjoyed in its original context, as an accompaniment to the dance. Highly recommended is Millicent Hodson and Kenneth Archer's version. These two ballet detectives reconstructed the original 1913 choreography by examining contemporary photographs and Nijinsky's Russian notes for the ballet. Their collaborative research resulted in a creative restoration of the work, as performed by dancers and musicians from the University of North Carolina School of the Arts. (You can view this performance today on YouTube.)

The opening measures of the piece, however, give little indication of the mood and action to follow. We hear soft and slow chords, first inching chromatically upward in the string and horn parts. The eerie mood then continues in the next few measures as the high first violin, celesta, and some of the winds enter with a languid falling motion that gently outline an augmented triad. This introduction is a gem. In just a few measures and with just a few notes, Debussy captures a mysterious twilight with the first stars appearing in the sky. In the process, he has set up an effective contrast to the faster, more abrupt changes that are about to take place when the dancers enter. He also arranges the introductory measures in such a way that they foreshadow the rest of the ballet. Listen to these opening measures again, noticing this time how the music falls into small (two- and four-bar) modules, with each consisting of a melodic idea that is repeated immediately, either exactly or with little variation. This modular design will be replicated throughout the unfolding of *Jeux* and is a good way for us to make sense of it. (Recall that we have seen Debussy's use of duplication before, such as in connection with *Pelléas et Mélisande* in chapter 3.)

The second section of the orchestral introduction (from 1:07 to 1:44) could not be more different. Here the tempo is marked *scherzando* (playful), the meter is in triple time (as compared to the previous quadruple time), and staccato sixteenth notes dominate. The instrumentation has changed as well. Whereas the first section featured the upper strings and winds, the ethereal harps and celesta, and echoing horn, the second section includes the bassoon, cellos and basses, and percussion instruments such as the cymbals, xylophone, and tambourine. This is not say that the additional instruments are used to thicken the music.

Rather, in keeping with the restless spirit of this contrasting section, the motives tend to flit from instrument to instrument so that the overall sound of the section is light and airy. Thus does Debussy foreshadow the pursuit that is about to ensue.

Also telling is the way he has designed the first two sections of music into adjacent but distinctive areas, each having its own sound and time. In effect, he has just presented a guiding principle for understanding all of *Jeux*: each section will have its own particular motive, rhythm, and timbre, whisking by in a seemingly disconnected manner to the next section. Let it not be forgotten, however, that Debussy was and always will be remembered as the structuralist par excellence. He would never take a haphazard approach to composition. In the case of *Jeux*, the strategy he chose was completely unprecedented. As explained by Pierre Boulez in *Stocktakings from an Apprenticeship* (1991), Debussy "braided" the sections of *Jeux* so that they are strung together:

> One must experience the whole work [*Jeux*] to have a grasp of its form, which is no longer architected, but braided; in other words, there is no distributive hierarchy in the organization of "sections" (static sections: themes; dynamic sections: developments) but successive distributions in the course of which the various constituent elements take on a greater or lesser functional importance. One can well understand that this sense of form is bound to run up against the listening habits formed by contact with three centuries of "architectural" music.

I cannot claim to hear all of the multiple threads between the sections because many of them are extremely subtle and tenuous. Yes, I can discern a pattern at work in *Jeux*: a motive, rhythm, or instrument will be rather hidden in one section but tends to emerge in the forefront in the next section. The reverse is also true, with ideas subsequently fading out of the limelight. In a sense, this refocusing of material reminds me of a cinematic technique called rack focus, which involves shifting the attention on one character or object to another.

I can also discern the existence of a poised equilibrium throughout *Jeux*. Descending lines often culminate in rising melodies. Upper strings playing smoothly may be followed by lower strings playing pizzicato. Soft passages are followed by loud sounds. We hear the high and then the low, the simple to the elaborate, and so on. This perfect balance of material prevents the constant back-and-forth motion from sounding choppy and enables the waves of sound to flow smoothly. Still, *Jeux* remains a challenging work to understand because there is an overabundance of material and detail; nothing ever returns exactly the same way as before, and the tempo is generally quick.

I will keep trying to decipher *Jeux*, using the action on stage as one of the keys to understanding the network of connections within the music. For example, three different meters map onto the three characters. The 3/8 and 3/4 meters are associated with the man and one of the women, who begin to dance together at 7:02. The second woman, fuming on the sidelines, interrupts them at 8:23, with a new and different 2/4 meter. The choice of key is also significant here. The man and the first woman dance in the key of F♯ major; when the second girl interrupts them, the key is C major. These two keys, which are diametrically opposed on the circle of fifths, underscore the rivalry between the characters.

Darmstadt and Beyond

Jeux was only initially a flop. It rose to greater prominence in the 1950s, due to the forward-looking attitudes of Pierre Boulez, Luigi Nono, Karlheinz Stockhausen, and other leading figures of the celebrated Darmstadt School. The courses there were intended to introduce German musicians to earlier modern music, which had been deemed "degenerate" under Hitler. Debussy's music for *Jeux* was one of those pieces that these postwar European composers rescued from obscurity and reintroduced. They were especially drawn to the work's unusual design, the subtle interrelationships between sections, and the constant renewal of material and color. Like Debussy, they were committed to creating new types of forms for their new music. They refused to write new music in outdated forms, which Boulez complained had been in use for three centuries. *Jeux* was an exemplar, one that "marked the arrival of a kind of musical form which, renewing itself from moment to moment, implies a similarly instantaneous mode of perception" (*Stocktakings*, 1991). Stockhausen, too, saw parallels between *Jeux* and his own "moment form," which describes a succession of formal units, each followed by a completed different formal unit.

Since the 1950s, *Jeux* has continued to resonate with younger gener-ations of composers. For Ellen Taaffe Zwilich, who in 1983 became the first woman to win the Pulitzer Prize in music, the significance of *Jeux* has yet to be fully appreciated: "I think *Jeux* is one of the most interest-ing pieces of the early 20th century. I find . . . that when the historical narrative is broadened, it will probably be seen as much more important than the *Rite of Spring*" (quoted in James Briscoe "The Resonance of Debussy for United States Post Modernists," 2014).

THE LEGACY CONTINUES

Jeux may not be a mainstream piece, but other works by Debussy are among the most beloved and performed to this day. His piano composi-tions, for example, are some of the foundation stones of the twentieth-century repertoire. The ones commonly appearing on student recital programs include *Rêverie* and the *Deux arabesques*; "The Girl with the Flaxen Hair" and "The Submerged Cathedral" from the first book of *Préludes*; "The Little Shepherd" and "Golliwog's Cakewalk" from *Chil-dren's Corner*; and "Clair de Lune" from the *Suite bergamasque*. Much more technically challenging are the *Douze Etudes*, *L'isle joyeuse*, *Es-tampes*, and the *Préludes* "Ce qu'a vu le vent d'ouest" and "Feux d'artifice."

Debussy's impact has been equally strong in popular culture. As stated at the very beginning of this book, his "Clair de Lune" has been reproduced, excerpted, and remixed as part of the soundtrack of so many different media. Typically, the work is heard in connection with infinite beauty. A case in point is *Frankie and Johnny in the Clair de Lune*, the 1987 play by Terrence McNally. Toward the end of story, Johnny calls a radio station to request "the most beautiful music in the world" so that "this thing" he and Frankie have will not destruct. Johnny himself does not know what that piece would be, but the DJ knows. In the next scene, he responds to Johnnie's request by playing Debussy's "Clair de Lune."

Yet Debussy's music, such as his *Arabesque* no. 1, has been used in unexpected and unusual ways as well. This simple but elegant piano piece stands out as one of only two instances of audible music in *The Birds*, Alfred Hitchcock's 1963 thriller film. Melanie Daniels plays the

Arabesque after dinner at the Brenner house, a relaxed and peaceful scene. The second example of audible music in the film is a cheerful, nonsensical folk song called "Risselty-Rosselty" that the schoolchildren sing at a much later point in the movie. All other sounds in the movie, including bird noises, were generated electronically, perhaps to symbolize the inhumanity of the birds.

In both of these scenes Hitchcock uses the music in a similar way, namely, as an effective foil to contrast with and heighten tension. During the "Risselty-Rosselty" scene, the children sing the many verses of the tune in a bizarre counterpoint to the birds silently gathering and lining up outside the classroom, ready to make a coordinated strike. Sure enough, the flock of angry birds attacks the children shortly after they leave the school. As for the after-dinner scene with the Debussy music, the simultaneous juxtaposition between relaxation and tension involves Melanie, who has a crush on Mitch Brenner, and his lonely, clinging mother. While Melanie plays the delicate *Arabesque* on a spinet piano in the living room, Lydia Brenner is grilling Mitch about Melanie's past in the kitchen. Her anxiety about losing her son to Melanie is palpable.

Today, in the twenty-first century, interest in Debussy has exploded as a result of a popular sci-fi western series on HBO called *Westworld*. Based on a 1973 film created by Michael Crichton of *Jurassic Park* fame, it features cowboy and cowgirl robots instead of dinosaurs. The lifelike robots are called hosts, and they exist to engage in multiple story lines, or narratives, with wealthy human guests. A huge part of *Westworld*'s appeal is its construction, which is essentially a whole series of puzzles and clues, but the music is also key to the series' success. During the ten episodes of season 1, which aired in the fall of 2016, the music ran the gamut from classical to rock. Examples of covers and arrangements included Bizet's "Habanera," Tchaikovsky's music for *Swan Lake*, Debussy's "Clair de Lune," the Rolling Stones' "Paint It Black," Radiohead's "Fake Plastic Trees," and Amy Winehouse's "Back to Black."

Apart from the main theme, written by Ramin Djawadi, the music that recurred most often throughout season 1 was Debussy's *Rêverie* (Daydream) for piano. In a remarkable way, it was an aural clue that functioned along the lines of a visual clue. At first, a visual clue will appear as a small detail, one that might be easily overlooked. Over time, it gradually develops into a fuller event or explanation. Recall, for instance, the ending of episode 1, "The Original," when the host Dolores kills a fly, even though we have been informed that hosts are incapable of hurting living things. At the end of season 1, Delores appears to have killed Dr. Ford, a human and one of the original creators of the *Westworld* theme park. Subsequently, at the beginning of season 2, which is currently airing, she slaughters multiple guests to the sound of Scott Joplin's *Entertainer*.

Rêverie follows a similar trajectory. When it is introduced in episode 3, "The Stray," we hear just a tiny snippet of the music, here serving as a perfect accompaniment to Ford's flashback scene. The piece recurs twice in episode 7, "Trompe L'Oeil," first at the beginning of the episode and then during the closing credits; each of these recurrences consists of longer segments that are more audible. In episode 8, "Trace Decay," *Rêverie* reappears just once, but significantly its function seems to have changed: it is now used to calm down or perhaps control a host (in this case, Maeve). Episode 9, "The Well-Tempered Clavier," features multiple and even longer portions of *Rêverie*, often in alternation with Djawadi's original theme. In a sense, there are strong parallels between the music and the scenes. We hear the Debussy whenever Bernard is having flashbacks of his son's death, whereas we hear the theme song of the series when Bernard comes to realize that his son's death was a lie—he never even existed. In fact, Bernard is not even real. In the final episode, "The Bicameral Mind," *Rêverie* again recurs multiple times, including the warped version emanating from an old Victrola. In short, the meaning of Debussy's *Rêverie* has evolved over the course of season 1 of *Westworld*, at first representing a daydream and later acting as a code for tranquilizing and updating the robots. At the conclusion of episode 10, we finally learn an important truth: "the reveries" are essential to the hosts as a gateway for remembering past narratives and suffering, thereby becoming more human.

It is ironic that *Westworld*'s production team settled on Debussy's *Rêverie* of 1890 as an essential component of their narrative. He himself disliked this piece, which he deemed unworthy of publication because it did not compare to his more serious and innovative music. In a 1904 letter to the publisher Fromont, he complained: "I regret very much your decision to publish Reverie . . . . I wrote it in a hurry many years ago, purely for material considerations. It is a work of no consequence and I frankly consider it no good." Yet the team made a fitting choice because the music sometimes associated with amusement parks is commercial and culturally "cheap" with low artistic value.

I think there is another lesson to be learned here: Debussy's music, be it high or low art, is constructed to last.

SELECTED LISTENING

Claude Debussy: Préludes. Krystian Zimerman. Deutsche Grammophon. Recorded 1991, released 1994. 435773.

Debussy: Images; Prélude à l'après-midi d'un faune; Printemps. Cleveland Orchestra. Conducted by Pierre Boulez. Deutsche Grammophon. Released 1993. 435766.

Debussy: Images; 2 Arabesques; L'isle joyeuse; Berceuse héroïque. Zoltán Kocsis. Philips. CD released 1990. 422404 (includes *Rêverie, Hommage à Haydn,* and *D'un cahier d'esquisses*).

Debussy: La mer; Nocturnes; Jeux; Rhapsodie pour clarinette et orchestra. Cleveland Orchestra. Conducted by Pierre Boulez. Deutsche Grammophon. Released 1995. 439896.

Debussy: Mélodies. Mady Mesplé, Gérard Souzay, Frederica von Stade, Elly Ameling, Michèle Command, Dalton Baldwin. EMI Classics. Recorded 1971–1979, CD released 1992. 7640952.

Debussy: Pelléas et Mélisande. Richard Stilwell, Frederica von Stade, José van Dam, Ruggero Raimondi, Nadine Denize. Berlin Philharmonic. Conducted by Herbert von Karajan. EMI Classics. Recorded 1978, CD released 2009. 66723.

Debussy: Suite bergamasque; Pour le piano; Estampes; Images (oubliées). Zoltán Kocsis. Philips. Recorded 1983, CD released 1990. 412118.

Debussy: String Quartet in G Minor; op. 10 String Quartet. Emerson String Quartet. Deutsche Grammophon. Recorded 1986, CD released 1995. 445509 (with Ravel's String Quartet).

Debussy: 3 Sonatas; Syrinx. Arthur Grumiaux, Maurice Gendron, Roger Bourdin. Philips Classics. Recorded in 1960s, CD released 1989. 422839 (includes String Quartet in G minor, op. 10).

Debussy: 12 Etudes. Maurizio Pollini. Deutsche Grammophon. Recorded 1992, released 1994. 423678 (with Berg's Sonata op. 1).

Debussy: Works for Two Pianos and Piano Four Hands. Claude Helffer and Haakon Austbö. Harmonia Mundi. Recorded 1973, CD released 1990. 190957 (includes *En blanc et noir, Lindaraja, Marche écossaise sur un thème populaire, Petite suite,* and *Épigraphes antiques*).

SELECTED READING

Abbate, Carolyn. *"Tristan* in the Composition of *Pelléas." 19th-Century Music* 5, no. 2 (Autumn 1981): 117–41.

Blanche, Jacques-Emile. *La Pêche aux souvenirs.* Paris: Flammarion, 1949.

Boulez, Pierre. *Orientations: Collected Writings.* Edited by Jean-Jacques Nattiez. Translated by Martin Cooper. Cambridge, MA: Harvard University Press, 1986.

———. *Stocktakings from an Apprenticeship.* Edited by Paule Thevenin. Translated by Stephen Walsh. Oxford: Oxford University Press, 1991.

Bourion, Sylveline. *Le style de Claude Debussy: Duplication, repetition et dualité dans les strategies de composition.* Paris: Vrin, 2001.

Branger, Jean-Christophe. "La réponse de Debussy à une enquête du Cri de Paris pendant la Grande Guerre." *Cahiers Debussy* 35 (2011): 97–108.

Briscoe, James. "The Resonance of Debussy for United States Post-Modernists." *Revue Musicale OICRM* 2, no. 1 (2014).

Brown, Matthew. *Debussy Redux: The Impact of His Music on Popular Culture, Musical Meaning and Interpretation.* Bloomington: Indiana University Press, 2012.

Carré, Albert. *Souvenirs de théâtre.* Edited by Robert Favart. Paris: Plon, 1950.

Code, David. "Hearing Debussy Reading Mallarmé: Music *après Wagner* in the *Prélude à l'après-midi d'un faune." Journal of the American Musicological Society* 54, no. 3 (Fall 2001): 493–554.

———. "Parting the Veils of Debussy's *Voiles." Scottish Music Review* 1, no. 1 (2007). http://www.scottishmusicreview.org.

Debussy, Claude. *Correspondance (1872–1918).* Edited by François Lesure and Denis Herlin. Annotated by François Lesure, Denis Herlin, and Georges Liébert. Paris: Gallimard, 2005.

———. *Debussy Letters.* Edited by François Lesure and Roger Nichols. Translated by Roger Nichols. Cambridge, MA: Harvard University Press, 1987.

———. *Debussy on Music.* Edited by François Lesure. Translated by Richard Langham Smith. New York: Knopf, 1977.

———. *Monsieur Croche et autres écrits.* Edited by François Lesure. Paris: Gallimard, 1987.

Delaborde, Henri. "Rapport sur les envois de Rome en 1886." *Journal officiel* 18 (1886): 6082.

———. "Rapport sur les envois de Rome en 1887." *Journal officiel* 20 (1888): 977.

De Martelly, Elizabeth. "Signification, Objectification, and the Mimetic Uncanny in Claude Debussy's 'Golliwog's Cakewalk.'" *Current Musicology* 90 (Fall 2010): 7–34.

De Voto, Mark. *Debussy and the Veil of Tonality: Essays on His Music.* Hillsdale, NY: Pendragon, 2004.

Dietschy, Marcel. *A Portrait of Debussy*. Edited and translated by William Ashbook and Margaret G. Cobb. Oxford: Oxford University Press, 1990.

Doret, Gustave. *Temps et contretemps: Souvenirs d'un musicien*. Fribourg: Librairie de l'Université, 1942.

Dumesnil, Maurice. *Claude Debussy: Master of Dreams*. New York: Ives Washburn, 1940.

Durand, Jacques. *Quelques souvenirs d'un Éditeur de musique*, vol. 2, *1910–1924*. Paris: Durand, 1925.

Fauser, Annegret. *Musical Encounters at the 1889 Paris World's Fair*. Rochester, NY: University of Rochester Press, 2005.

Fulcher, Jane. *The Composer as Intellectual: Music and Ideology in France, 1914–1940*. Oxford: Oxford University Press, 2005.

———, ed. *Debussy and His World*. Princeton, NJ: Princeton University Press, 2001.

———. "Debussy as National Icon: From Vehicle of Vichy's Compromise to French Resistance Classic." *The Musical Quarterly* 94, no. 4 (2011): 454–80.

Grayson, David. "The Libretto of Debussy's '*Pelléas et Mélisande*.'" *Music and Letters* 66, no. 1 (January 1985): 34–50.

Herlin, Denis. "An Artist High and Low; or, Debussy and Money." In *Rethinking Debussy*, edited by Elliott Antokoletz and Marianne Wheeldon, 149–202. New York: Oxford University Press, 2011.

Holloway, Robin. *Debussy and Wagner*. London: Eulenberg, 1979.

Howat, Roy. "Debussy and the Orient." In *Recovering the Orient: Artists, Scholars, Appropriations*, edited by Andrew Gerstle and Anthony Milner, 45–82. London: Routledge, 1995.

———. *Debussy in Proportion: A Musical Analysis*. Cambridge: Cambridge University Press, 1983.

Kelly, Barbara L. "Debussy and the Making of a *musicien français*: *Pelléas*, the Press, and World War I." In *French Music, Culture, and National Identity, 1870–1939*, edited by Barbara L. Kelly, 69–97. Rochester, NY: University of Rochester Press, 2008.

———. *Music and Ultra-Modernism in France: A Fragile Consensus, 1913–1939*. Woodbridge, UK: Boydell, 2013.

———. "Ravel after Debussy: Inheritance, Influences and Style." In *Berlioz and Debussy: Sources, Contexts and Legacies: Essays in Honour of François Lesure*, edited by Barbara L. Kelly and Kerry Murphy, 181–92. Aldershot, UK: Ashgate, 2007.

Laloy, Louis. *Claude Debussy*. Paris: Dorbon Ainé, 1909.

Langham Smith, Richard, and Roger Nichols. *Pelléas et Mélisande*. Cambridge: Cambridge University Press, 1989.

Lesure, François. *Catalogue de l'oeuvre de Claude Debussy*. Geneva: Minkoff, 1977.

———. *Claude Debussy: Biographie critique*. Paris: Klincksieck, 1994.

———. *Claude Debussy avant Pelléas ou les années symbolistes*. Paris: Klincksieck, 1993.

———. "Correspondence de Claude Debussy et de Louis Laloy (1902–1914)." *Revue de Musicologie* 48, no. 125 (1962): 3–40.

———. "'L'affaire' Debussy-Ravel: Lettres inédities." In *Festschrift Friedrich Blume*, edited by Anna Amalie Abert and Wilhelm Pfannkuch, 231–34. Kassel, Germany: Bärenreiter, 1963.

———. "Ravel et Debussy." *Cahiers Maurice Ravel* 5 (1992): 27–33.

Lockspeiser, Edward. *Debussy: His Life and Mind*. 2nd ed. Cambridge: Cambridge University Press, 1978.

———. "Debussy, Tchaikovsky and Madame von Meck," *The Musical Quarterly* 22, no. 1 (1936): 38–44.

———. "Neuf lettres de Pierre Louys a Debussy (1894–98)." *Revue de Musicologie* 48, no. 125: 61–71.

Marnat, Marcel. Maurice Ravel. Paris: Fayard, 1986.

McCombie, Elizabeth. *Mallarmé and Debussy: Unheard Music, Unseen Text*. Oxford: Oxford University Press, 2003.

Murakami, Hitomi. "On the Formation of Images of Musical Impressionism as Found in the Writings of Literary Men and Musical Critics in Japan of the Prewar Period." *Journal of*

Cultural Studies in Body, Design, Media, Music and Text 3, no. 1 (November 2001): 37–50.

Nichols, Roger. *Debussy*. Oxford: Oxford University Press, 1973.

———. *Debussy Remembered*. London: Faber, 1992.

———. *The Life of Debussy*. Cambridge: Cambridge University Press, 1998.

———. *Ravel*. New Haven, CT: Yale University Press, 2011.

Orenstein, Arbie. *Ravel: Man and Musician*. New York: Columbia University Press, 1975.

———, trans. and ed. *A Ravel Reader: Correspondence, Articles, Interviews*. New York: Dover, 2003.

Orledge, Robert. "Debussy the Man." In *The Cambridge Companion to Debussy*, edited by Simon Trezise, 9–24. Cambridge: Cambridge University Press, 2003.

———. *Satie the Composer*. Cambridge: Cambridge University Press, 1990.

Pasler, Jann. "Mélisande's Charm and the Truth of Her Music." In *Rethinking Debussy*, edited by Elliott Antokoletz and Marianne Wheeldon, 55–75. New York: Oxford University Press, 2011.

———. "*Pelléas* and Power: Forces behind the Reception of Debussy's Opera." *19th-Century Music* 10, no. 3 (Spring 1987): 243–64.

———. "A Sociology of the Apaches: 'Sacred Battalion' for Pelléas." In *Berlioz and Debussy: Sources, Contexts, Legacies*, edited by Barbara L. Kelly and Kerry Murphy, 149–66. Aldershot, UK: Ashgate, 2007.

Penesco, Anne, ed. *Etudes sur la musique française: Autour de Debussy, Ravel et Paul Le Flem*. Lyon, France: Presses Universitaires, 1914.

Petrova, Anna. "La réception de Debussy à Saint-Pétersbourg au début du vingtième siècle." *Cahiers Debussy* 25 (2001): 11–63.

Philipp, Isidor, and Frederick H. Martens. "The French National Conservatory of Music." *The Musical Quarterly* 6, no. 2 (April 1920): 214–26.

Priest, Deborah, trans. and ed. *Louis Laloy (1874–1944) on Debussy, Ravel, and Stravinsky*. Aldershot, UK: Ashgate, 1999.

Rolland, Romain, ed. *Richard Strauss et Romain Rolland: Correspondance, fragments de journal*. *Cahiers Romain Rolland* 3 (1951): 154–65.

Rosen, Charles. "Influence: Plagiarism and Inspiration." *19th-Century Music* 4, no. 2 (Autumn 1980): 87–100.

Ruwet, Nicolas. "Note sur les duplications dans l'oeuvre de Claude Debussy." *Revue Belge de Musicologie* 16, no. 1/4 (1962): 57–70.

Schmalfeldt, Janet. "Form as the Process of Becoming: The Beethoven-Hegelian Tradition and the Tempest Sonata." *Beethoven Forum* 4 (1995): 37–71.

Trezise, Simon. "Debussy's 'Rhythmicised Time.'" In *The Cambridge Companion to Debussy*, edited by Simon Trezise, 232–55. Cambridge: Cambridge University Press, 2003.

———. *La mer*. Cambridge: Cambridge University Press, 1995.

Tymoczko, Dmitri. "Scale Networks and Debussy." *Journal of Music Theory* 48, no. 2 (Fall 2004): 219–94.

Vallas, Léon. *Claude Debussy: His Life and Works*. Trans. by Marie and Grace O'Brien. Oxford: Oxford University Press, 1933.

Vuillermoz, Émile. *Histoire de la musique*. Paris: Fayard, 1949.

Wheeldon, Marianne. "Debussy and La Sonate cyclique." *Journal of Musicology* 2, no. 4 (Fall 2005): 644–79.

———. *Debussy's Late Style*. Indianapolis: Indiana University Press, 2017.

———. *Debussy's Legacy and the Construction of Reputation*. Oxford: Oxford University Press, 2017.

Woldu, Gail Hilson, and Sophie Queuniet. "Au-delà du scandale de 1905: Propos sur le Prix de Rome au début du xxᵉ siècle." *Revue de Musicologie* 82, no. 2 (1996): 245–67.

Zank, Stephen. *Irony and Sound: The Music of Maurice Ravel*. Rochester, NY: University of Rochester Press, 2009.

INDEX

ABOUT THE AUTHOR

Theorist, musicologist, and pianist **Teresa Davidian** specializes in French and American music of the late nineteenth and twentieth centuries. Her research areas include the music of Claude Debussy and Ruth Crawford Seeger, and her articles have appeared in *The Musical Quarterly*, the *Journal of Music Theory Pedagogy*, *Notes*, the *Journal of Musicological Research*, *Theory and Practice*, and *Bluegrass Now*. Her previous book for Rowman & Littlefield is *Tonal Counterpoint for the 21st-Century Musician: An Introduction*. Davidian is professor of music at Tarleton State University in Texas, a member of the Texas A&M University System.

www.ingramcontent.com/pod-product-compliance
Lightning Source LLC
Chambersburg PA
CBHW020357100426
42812CB00001B/92